I0025528

LEGALLY HAUNTED

Dylan Clearfield

ISBN 978-0-930472-75-7

Copyright © 2023 Prism Thomas

All rights reserved

Second revised edition

EDITED IN NEWPORT, WALES (British spelling applies)

Opening statement

Part 1 - Homicides

Part 2 - Haunted Houses

Part 3 - Wills, Treasures and photographs

All cases are genuine and documented.

OPENING STATEMENT

Do ghosts exist? Their reality has been challenged by various courts of law throughout the world. Trials have been held, witnesses have testified, and judges and juries have rendered decisions concerning the existence of ghosts.

The first volume of this three volume work entitled *GHOSTS IN COURT* examines murder cases in which the ghosts of the victims have taken active parts in bringing to justice the person or persons who killed them. Every case is true and fully documented. Most of the documentation is in the form of official court records.

FORM OF PRESENTATION

Each case will be dealt with individually and will be issued an unofficial docket number purely for identification within the scope of this work. The information supplied to the right gives the primary source used for the information that follows. However, since several sources were consulted for each docketed case only the primary source will be listed.

Each docketed case will be presented in three parts. The first part will be an abstract of the case in which the basic elements of the issues involved will be described.

The second part will consist of an examination of the facts and the witnesses. Witnesses will usually be quizzed in a deposition format or as questioning would have occurred in a courtroom. Even though the transcripts no longer exist in most cases, what will be presented **WILL CONSIST OF FACTUAL EVIDENCE AND NOTHING WILL BE CONJECTURE OR SPECULATION.** All of the information brought forward will be from official court records and other legal documents.

The third part of the presentation will be delivery of the verdict. All verdicts will be the true and actual findings of the court or other legal body that held jurisdiction over the hearings.

Everything in this volume and the two that follow is factual and fully documented! Citations will be provided so that you may examine the documents yourself. You will need access to an excellent law library, however, because most of the cases are rare, not contemporary, and often outside the American or English system of jurisprudence. But they are all legal and valid. And keep in mind, the final version of each case is a melding together of information gleaned from several sources. Some sources were given more weight than others.

This is a book about ghosts and ghost stories. It is also a book about how ghosts have directly interacted with the legal system. By directly it is meant that the ghosts themselves have made appearances in various settings. **This is NOT a book about psychic detectives or so-called crime-solving mediums!** It IS about ghosts and their impact on the legal system through direct intervention.

PART 1 - HOMICIDES

C.T. Stewart was murdered as the result of a nefarious conspiracy. The method of his murder was by strychnia poisoning and the motive for his killing was to collect insurance money upon Mr. Stewart's demise.

The men who took part in the conspiracy were Guy jack and (Herbert) (sic) Lipscomb, a medical MD.

· POINT OF PRIMARY SIGNIFICANCE: *it would have been impossible for the murdered man - C. T. Stewart - to have known about the conspiracy to kill him without some form of supernatural intervention acquired after his death.*

C.T. Stewart was very ill, but his condition was such that he might have lingered for many years. Doctor Lipscomb had been treating him for many months and had been able to maintain the young man's condition, but not improve it. Guy Jack was a friend of the doctor's and was aware of the situation with Mr. Stewart. Guy had a plan.

Guy Jack's plan was to take out a hefty insurance policy on Mr. Stewart in his own name to avoid suspicion and then to have Dr. Lipscomb poison his own patient. This was 1897, a time when honest physicians truly worked for altruistic reasons rather than for the prospect of becoming wealthy and when malpractice suits were things of the distant future. Doctor Lipscomb was more interested in becoming wealthy than in healing the sick and so he agreed to Guy jack's plan.

Why didn't the doctor simply murder Mr. Stewart himself and collect the entire insurance payment? Because it would've looked *very* suspicious for an attending physician to collect the insurance payment on his dead patient - even in 1897! So Guy Jack purchased the policy and Dr. Lipscomb administered the poison. It was impossible for C.T. Stewart to know about this arrangement before his death.

The plan seemed foolproof. The doctor visited his patient as normal and, instead of giving him his medication, he administered to him a capsule laced with the deadly poison, strychnnine. But neither Guy Jack nor Dr. Lipscomb could have anticipated ghostly interference - from the newly deceased!

There were two witnesses to the appearance of the deceased's ghost while still on his deathbed, one of them the wife of C.T. Stewart. She described the scene in court and the following is a simulation of her testimony. **Note: all of the basic facts are true and intact.**

PROSECUTOR TO MRS. STEWART

Q. What is your relation to the deceased?

A. I am - I was - his wife.

Q. Were you with him on the night of his death?

A. Yes, I was.

Q. Was there anyone else in the room with you at the time that your husband expired?

A. Yes, my man, Jasper.

Q. Did he see the events that occurred that evening?

A. Yes. He was there the entire time.

Q. Can you tell us in your own words - Mrs. Stewart - what happened on the night of your husband's murder?

A. Doctor Lipscomb came by around six o'clock in the evening. My husband had a distressful day and I asked the doctor if he could do something to relieve the congestion my husband was suffering from.

Q. Did the doctor oblige?

A. Well, yes. He did all the usual tests he does and then reached into his bag for a special pill.

Q. Special? Why do you characterise it as special?

A. It wasn't like the other pills. It was - uh, he called it a capsule. It was red, not like the others.

Q. What happened after your husband took the capsule?

A. You mean later?

Q. Later?

A. Yes. The doctor gave me the capsule and told me to give it to my husband at bedtime. Then the doctor left.

Q. I see. Was your man - Jasper - there when the doctor gave you the capsule?

A. Yes. Like I said, Jasper was there the whole time. He saw him give me the red capsule.

Q. Then later that night your husband took the capsule?

A. Yes at bedtime, around nine o'clock.

Q. And Jasper was there to witness this, too?

4

A. The whole time.

Q. Anyone else?

A. No.

Q. What happened after your husband took the capsule?

A. Nothing at first. He just laid back and we tried to make him comfortable.

Q When did he start showing effects from taking the capsule?

A. Ten, maybe fifteen minutes later.

Q. Can you describe how he reacted?

A. I'll never forget it. He got all wild about the eyes, threw his arms into the air, looked all cramped up and in great pain.

Q. Did you do anything for him?

A. We gave him some whiskey and coffee.

Q. What effect did that have?

A. It didn't seem to have any. He just got worse. Started to have convulsions.

Q. What ultimately happened to your husband?

A. He had a final convulsion and...died.

Q. Was that the end of it?

A. No. No. He revived - or it was his ghost or something.

Q. Revived from the dead?

A. Yes. That's what he himself said.

Q. Your husband?

A. Yes! His exact words were: '*I have been dead and the Lord sent me back to tell you that Dr. Lipscomb poisoned me with a capsule he gave me to-night. Guy Jack had my life insured, and he hired Dr. Lipscomb to kill me.*'

Q. You're certain, absolutely certain, that that's what he said?

A. His exact words. Jasper will tell you the same.

Q. And your husband had...died?

A. Yes. He was already dead.

Q. How can you possibly be certain he was dead? That is an extraordinary claim.

A. For one thing, he had no signs of life.

Q. Maybe so. But sometimes the signs of life can be so faint that a trained physician can even be fooled.

A. There's something else. Something foolproof to show he was dead.

Q. What would that be?

A. My husband knew about the conspiracy to murder him. He told us about it, that's how we knew that he was murdered. How could he possibly have known about the plan to murder him if he hadn't passed to the other world and been told this information there?

_____

_____

This was evidence that could not be denied. How else could the deceased possibly have known about the conspiracy if not through paranormal means!

Even as astounding as this was his announcing that it was the Lord who sent him back to see that justice was served! The Lord would be Jesus Christ Himself - in the afterlife.

But would any of this be accepted by the court? The proposals seemed preposterous. There was only one way to verify the charges that had been leveled by the ghost of the deceased: prove the existence of the insurance policy in question and all of the particulars associated with it. If this were done, there could be no other choice than to accept as true the assertions of the ghost.

_____

An investigation was made. All of the assertions made by the ghost of C.T. Stewart were checked and verified. The policy was drawn up by Guy Jack just days before the demise of Mr. Stewart! There could be only one finding by the court - guilty!

This was the verdict of the court not once but twice. The original finding of guilt was appealed and the verdict was upheld by the higher court.

- **OFFICIAL VERDICT:** *Guy Jack and Dr. Lipscomb were both convicted of conspiracy to commit murder and the murder itself. Both men were condemned to death. Doctor Lipscomb died in prison before the sentence could be carried out, and Guy Jack disappeared.*

MORE

Vital to note is that - in addition to discovery of the existence of the damning insurance policy - the court accepted the deceased's remarks as a deathbed declaration and as such it was admissible as evidence. Deathbed declarations are commonly accepted in legal proceedings as true statements. This means that C.T. Stewart's assertion that he had come back from the dead with a message given to him by The Lord was a factual statement.

The implications are **profound!** It was C.T. Stewart's ghost that returned after he'd died, therefore the court **acknowledged the reality of ghosts**. But in addition to this, the court also **acknowledged the existence of Jesus Christ** - the Lord - in the world beyond for how else could C.T. Stewart's spirit have returned with the information it had?

The next entry will be somewhat familiar to most people who are interested in ghosts and spiritualism because it involves the famous Fox sisters, the two girls who revived modern spiritualism in 1848.

Most people are familiar with the story of the ghostly knocking with which Katie and Margaret Fox established intelligent communication. But for some reason very few people are wholly unaware of the other event of legal importance which occurred in the Fox household at the same time.

The commission of a brutal murder was uncovered. A crime that was revealed by a

During one of their séances, the Fox sisters were contacted by the ghost of Mr. Rosma and he revealed to them the circumstances surrounding his murder. The information that was forthcoming was considerable so reliable that a formal inquest was held.

· **POINT OF PRIMARY SIGNIFICANCE:** *the ghost of the murdered man made*

ghost!

Several years before the Foxes moved into their now famous house in Hydesville, New York it was occupied by a family named the Johnsons (changed for privacy reasons). A traveling salesman named Charles B. Rosma appeared at the Johnson's home one day, and was never seen alive again.

direct contact with a large group of people during the séance and it was from his information that hard evidence was later discovered. Until this time, no one had even suspected that any wrongdoing had occurred.

The ghostly information was gleaned by a painstaking letter by letter identification process. A letter of the alphabet was called out and when the correct one was spoken, the spirit rapped in response. Armed with a notepad, another person would write down the letter and in a step-by-step fashion eventually knit together a comprehensible message.

Following is what one of these communications would have sounded like. **Note: all of the information contained in this section is factual.**

BY THE MEDIUM

Q. What is your name?

A. Charles B. Rosma.

Q. What was the highest age you attained while living upon the earth?

A. Thirty-one years.

Q. What was your occupation?

A. salesman.

Q. Did you have a family?

A. Yes. A wife and five children.

++

Q. Are you the cause of the rapping that has been heard in this house?

A. Some of it, yes.

Q. What message are you trying to convey?

A. I was murdered.

Q. Murdered?

A. Yes.

Q. By whom?

A. The man who lived here before.

Q. Before what?

A. Before those who live here now.

Q. The Johnsons lived here before the Foxes.

A. Yes.

Q. You were murdered by one of the Johnsons?

A. Yes.

Q. What happened to your body?

A. It was buried.

==

Q. Where?

A. In the cellar.

Q. The cellar in this house, what used to be the Johnson's house?

A. Yes. Ten feet under the surface.

It was this information which led to the formal inquest. However, even before the inquest was convened an excavation was made in the cellar. David Fox - older brother of Margaret and Kate - did most of the digging.

When David reached the five foot mark below the surface he came upon the remains of a suspicious wooden plank. He continued digging and almost immediately loosened shards of pottery and bits of charcoal. A little bit deeper and he found the telltale signs of a hasty burial - quicklime.

The purpose of quicklime is to speed up the disintegration of a buried body. Not surprisingly, human remains were found mixed in with the quicklime. Was it the remains of Mr. Rosma?

This became the reason for the inquest - identification of the remains. The presiding coroner called as one of his main witnesses a young woman named Lucretia Pulver. Lucretia had worked as housekeeper for the Johnsons. Her testimony was particularly interesting as it is here recalled substantially as it occurred. All information is factual.

BY THE CORNONER

Q. State your name please.

A. Lucretia Pulver.

Q. As I understand it, you were a housekeeper for the Johnsons.

###

A. Yes, sir.

Q. Do you recall a time when a man named Charles Rosma came to the Johnsons home?

A. Yes, sir.

Q. Why was he there?

A. He was a traveling salesman.

Q. Do you recall anything unusual about his visit?

A. Yes. The Johnsons asked him to stay the night.

Q. Why do you consider that unusual?

A. Well, they weren't what I would call sociable people.

Q. How often did you do housecleaning for the Johnsons?

A. I'd stop by everyday during the week. Mostly did just touch up cleaning. That's why I was surprised when I was told not to come back for three days after Mr. Rosma stayed.

Q. I don't understand. What do you mean?

A. He came on a weekday, not a Friday, you know. So I expected to come back the next few days for my regular cleaning. But I was told not to come back for at least three days.

Q. Were you told why?

A. No, sir. They didn't usually tell me nothing.

Q. Did you eventually return to the Johnsons house?

A. Yes, sir. Went back to my cleaning.

Q. Was Mr. Rosma there?

A. No, sir.

Q. How was the environment in the house when you returned? What I mean is - was anything different?

A. Yes. The house had a strange sort of feel to it. And there were the noises.

Q. Noises?

A. Yes. From the cellar. Very strange noises.

Q. Did the Johnsons hear these noises, too?

A. Yes. They told me it was rats.

Q. Did you ever go down into the cellar?

A. Yes. I'd been down there before but it was different now.

Q. Different? How?

A. The dirt in the middle of the cellar floor was soft. As if it had been dug up.

Q. Did you ask the Johnsons about this?

A. Yes, they said it was caused by rats digging.

Soon after the noises began, the Johnsons moved out and Lucretia lost her job. The next family to move in was named the Weekmans but they didn't stay very long. The noises forced them to leave. The next owners were the Foxes.

As the inquest continued, Mr. Johnson was called to testify. He was basically unresponsive to all of the questions, disavowing knowledge of any of the unusual activities that Lucretia had described.

Unfortunately, a positive identification of the remains in the cellar could not be made. The major problem was the inability to locate any such person as Charles B. Rosma having ever existed. Neither his wife nor children could be positively located, either.

Why not? If the information was supplied by a spirit, the ghost of the deceased, why wasn't the data verifiable?

The occasional unreliability of spirit information is a common problem in the field of psychic research. This doesn't necessarily imply dishonesty on the part of the spirit. The explanation more likely is simple confusion.

Confusion? Most people would agree that death can be a profound experience. The psyche can remain in a state of shock for a lengthy period, even causing temporary confusion of personal identity.

In the case of the spirit of Mr. Rosma the confusion could be a matter of a simple letter confused with another or interchanged. Maybe the true name in life was Rimsa, or any other combination of letters.

At any rate, the result of the inquest was indecisive.

· **OFFICIAL VERDICT:** *using information provided by a ghost, the remains of a human body were discovered in the cellar of a home belonging to the Fox family of Hydesville, New York. Identification of the remains could not be made, however. Proper burial was made.*

DOCKET # A3 (1745) CASE AND COMMENT, 454

Arthur Davies was a member of one of the British garrisons left in Scotland following the repression of the revolt of Prince Charlie. He was murdered by two local citizens. His ghost appeared to another local citizen and harassed him until his body was buried and the murderers were brought to trial.

- **POINT OF PRIMARY SIGNIFICANCE:** *in an exceptionally rare occurrence two people witnessed the same ghost at the same time from different locations. The ghost belonged to the murdered Sergeant Davies in his continued attempt to secure justice for himself.*

---

he took these valuables with him into the wilderness.

At any rate, Sergeant Davies was never seen alive again.

Alexander MacPherson was a Scotsman who lived in the area where General Guise's Regiment was barracked and was accustomed to taking walks through the countryside. One day in 1745 he encountered a most extraordinary sight.

A satisfactory answer to the first observation has not yet been obtained. But the reason that ghosts often appear only many years after their passing is that it takes many spirits that long to come to the realisation that they are no longer living on the earthly plane. Death when sudden and tragic is not always immediately recognised and understood by the newly deceased.

Arthur Davies was one of those military men who'd been left behind in Scotland to make sure that the idea of revolt did not stir again. He'd been a sergeant in General Guises's Regiment of Foot. On September 28, 1749 Sergeant Davies left his camp for a hike alone through the hills, wearing a number of gold rings and carrying a bagful of gold. It isn't clear why

Coming upon him, dressed in his blue uniform, was the ghost of Sergeant Davies.

Important to note at this point are two idiosyncrasies of ghosts: 1) when needing help they often appear to total strangers and, 2) they often make their first appearance several years after they had passed on.

Thus the series of events: the ghost of Davies appears to Mr. MacPherson, beckoning him to follow; McPherson follows, at first thinking that the ghost is actually the brother of a friend of his, an attorney named Farquharson; the ghost stops, points to a spot directly ahead of them and announces, 'I am the ghost of Arthur Davies,' then vanishes.

MacPherson proceeds forward and notices a badly decomposed body lying mostly hidden under chunks of peat, rock and rotted vegetation. MacPherson does nothing. He does not attend to the body and does not tell anyone about his meeting with the ghost. The disappearance of Arthur Davies was common knowledge, but the Scotsman didn't want to get involved in the murder of a British soldier.

This only made the ghost furious and initiated a second visit to MacPherson a few days later. This time it was in a type of communal building called the sheiling which MacPherson shared with a woman named Isobel McHardie.

Both MacPherson and McHardie were in the process of settling down for bed when the ghost rammed through the front

---

Following is a sample rendering of the deposition with its factual content intact.

BY THE PROSECUTOR
Q. State your name please.
A. Donald Farquharson.
Q. What is your occupation?
A. I am a barrister.
Q. Are you familiar with the events concerning the disappearance of Sergeant Arthur Davies?
A. I am.
Q. Did you recently have a discussion with Alexander MacPherson concerning the murder of Arthur Davies?
A. Yes, I did.
Q. Did Mr. MacPherson state that he was visited by the ghost of the murdered man?
A. Yes, he did.

Q. Did he state that the ghost divulged to him the location of the murdered man's body?
A. He did.
Q. Was the body subsequently located at the location that was specified?
A. It was.
Q. Did the ghost reveal the identity of its murderers?
A. Yes, the names it gave were Duncan Terig, also known as Duncan Clerk, and Alexander Bain MacDonald.
Q. Did the ghost offer particulars of its murder?
A. Yes, the spirit of Davies told MacPherson that he was shot to death on Christies Hill at the head of Glenconie by Terig or MacDonald.
Q. I understand that there is some information of your own that you would

like to offer at this time.

A. Yes. Some time ago, after the date when Davies was murdered, I noticed that the wife of Terig was wearing on her fingers a couple of the golden rings which I have since discovered belonged to the murdered man.

Q. Have you personally seen the ghost of Arthur Davies?

A. No, sir. But MacPherson told me that his roomate, Isobel McHardie witnessed the ghost.

_____

_____

Isobel McHardie was also deposed by Mr. McIntosh on the matter. Following is a sample rendering of her deposition with all of the factual material intact.

BY THE PROSECUTOR

Q. Now, discussing the night in question...

A. The night when I saw that fiend!

Q. Well, the ghost of Arthur Davies.

A. It was more like a creature from hell, it was.

Q. But it did identify itself as the spirit of Sergeant Arthur Davies?

A. Yes, sir. It was even wearing that old army cap of his, with the letters A. D. sewn on it. Otherwise it was an ugly, naked thing.

Q. Did you hear what the ghost said to Mr. Macpherson.

A. I'll never forget that horrible screeching sound.

Q. What language did he speak in?

A. Language? Huh, As good a Gaelic as I ever heard.

Q. You're aware of the deposition I took of Mr. Farquharson. Would you say that the things MacPherson said he heard the ghost say were what you heard?

A. Yes, sir. I heard the same thing.

Q. In Gaelic?

A. In Gaelic.

Despite all of the other facts in the case, the guilt or innocence of the defendants was determined by one thing and only one thing - the language the ghost has used!

The jury hearing the case discounted the fact that within weeks of the death of Davies, both Terig and MacDonald - who'd both been destitute - were each able to buy and stock a small farm. The gold that had been in Davies possession at the time of his murder would have provided just enough capital for such a venture.

The jury also discounted the fact that Mrs. Terig was seen wearing the rings that Davies was known to have had on his fingers at the time of his death.

What did the jury decide was the vital piece of evidence? The ghost's language. MacPherson himself was called to testify and after giving his accounts of the ghostly visitation, he was asked by the defendants' counsel: "And what language did the ghost speak to you in?"

MacPherson replied, "as good Gaelic as I'd ever heard in Lochaber."

To which the barrister replied with a scoff, "Pretty well, for the ghost of an English sergeant."

The point being: why would an English ghost speak Highland Gaelic instead of King's English.

· **OFFICIAL VERDICT:** *not guilty, because the jury did not believe that an English ghost would, or could, speak in Gaelic. Thus, a ghost returns to earth for justice and is thwarted. At least he did secure a proper burial for his body.*

A point to keep in mind when performing psychic investigation is that although a person has died and moved to another realm this does not necessarily mean he is now smarter, or stronger or in any other way improved upon what he had been. Death does not render a person omnipotent.

Thus, just because Arthur Davies had passed on to the other side does not necessarily mean he suddenly understood and could fluently speak Highland Gaelic.

However, nowhere in the records does it state that Mr. Davies DID NOT speak Highland Gaelic while living on this plane. He had been stationed in Scotland for more than a year and might have learned a great deal of the language. Also, the name Davies is generally a Welsh name. Might he not have been knowledgeable of other languages than the King's English?

Another major factor in this case was prejudice. How likely would it be for a Scottish jury to convict two local citizens for the murder of a British soldier? The matter of language was probably a convenient excuse.

%%%%%%%%%%%%%%%%%%%%%%%%%%%%%%%%%%%%%%%

A young Philippine nurse was brutally murdered in her apartment by a co-worker who was employed as an orderly at the same hospital. The ghost of the murder victim repeatedly appeared to her friend and ultimately testified through her in court in one of the most sensational spectacles in modern legal history.

· **POINT OF SIGNIFICANCE:** *the ghost spoke in court through her friend while the friend was under a trance and revealed facts about the crime that only the victim and the murderer could know.*

The names in the case have been changed because it is relatively recent even though it is in the public record and has been sensationalised in many forms of media. While undertaking independent research on the story I interviewed several of the peripheral participants who did not previously have the chance to offer their insights and they added many useful observations.

The deceased young woman will be identified as Carlotta and her friend through whom she communicated will be identified as Batiste. The murderer was a young black man named Howie.

There are two striking similarities between this case and the Arthur Davies murder. Language is one of them. In this case, both women were Philippine and both spoke the Tagalog dialect. The

ghost of Arthur Davies used Highland Gaelic in which to communicate with Mr. MacPherson.

Missing jewellery is also a vital component in the case of the murdered nurse as will shortly be noted.

Baptiste was employed as a respiratory therapist at a suburban hospital just outside of Chicago, Illinois. She had been working long hours and was exhausted.

Needing to take a little break from work, Baptiste went to the nurse's locker room and lay down on one of the benches.

There was no one else in the room at the time and she was enjoying the quiet. It was only a few days since the brutal murder of her acquaintance Carlotta and Baptiste was having difficulty resting. Although she and Carlotta had not been ghost of Arthur Davies used Highland Gaelic in which to communicate with Mr. MacPherson.

Missing jewellery is also a vital component in the case of the murdered nurse as will shortly be noted.

Baptiste was employed as a respiratory therapist at a suburban hospital just outside of Chicago, Illinois. She had been working long hours and was exhausted.

Needing to take a little break from work, Baptiste went to the nurse's locker room and lay down on one of the benches.

There was no one else in the room at the time and she was enjoying the quiet. It was only a few days since the brutal murder of her acquaintance Carlotta and Baptiste was having difficulty resting. Although she and Carlotta had not been close friends, Baptiste missed her and was still greatly distressed by her murder.

Suddenly, Baptiste became uneasy. Her rest was being disturbed by something she couldn't define and the young therapist abruptly awoke. Standing but a few feet from her was the ghost of Carlotta.

At this point somebody entered the room and the ghost vanished.

This was the first of a series of visits from the ghost of the murdered nurse. After this, Carlotta began appearing to Baptiste in her dreams.

Night after night Carlotta visited Baptiste in her sleep and re-enacted her slaying in nightmare form. Night after night Baptiste awoke screaming, also awaking her husband who was a medical doctor. She described the nightmares to him and asked if she should go to the authorities but he advised against it because she had no real proof.

Finally, Carlotta's ghost did provide proof. Once again through a dream, the spirit informed Baptiste that a piece of jewellery had been stolen from her by the murderer and that he had given it to his live-in girlfriend, Yanka as a belated Christmas present.

Of vital importance is the phone number that the ghost gave to Baptiste. It was the phone number of someone who could identify the jewellery, a cousin of its current owner. There was no other way that Baptiste could have gotten this phone number except by supernatural means.

• NOTE: *person's not familiar with psychic research may be confused as to why the ghost did not itself know the location of the girlfriend. Basically, it is because if the ghost did not know certain information while alive it would not have acquired this information - unless under unusual circumstances like with A.T. Stewart and his talk with the Lord - after passing on. Death does not automatically imbue special powers to the spirit.*

•

Now there was hard evidence to show the authorities. Baptiste took what she knew to the Evanston, Illinois police. They weren't interested, probably classifying the woman as a crank.

Baptiste would not give up so easily and made an appointment to see the district attorney directly. Since the murder case of Carlotta had gone very cold very quickly the D.A. decided he had nothing to lose so he listened to her.

The information he was given seemed reasonable so the district attorney obtained a search warrant and paid a visit to the home of the murderer's girlfriend. The jewellery in question was discovered and an arrest was quickly made.

Trial was set and was held at the Cook County Criminal Court Building in Chicago, Illinois in January of 1979. Presiding judge was Frank W. Sarbaro.

The primary witness in the case was Baptiste. When she was called to testify the direct examination began without incident, however, at a certain point the spirit of Carlotta took control of the witness. Following is a presentation of the questioning of Baptiste, with the factual information intact.

BY THE PROSECUTOR

Q. You were a friend of the deceased?

A. Yes, not close, but we often talked.

Q. It was information supplied by yourself that caused the defendant to be bound over for trial, was it not?

A. I believe so.

Q. You did bring knowledge of the stolen jewellery to the attention of the district attorney?

A. I did.

Q. How did this article of jewellery come into possession of the woman who had it?

A. It was given to her by the defendant.

Q. Were you there when he gave it to her?

A. No.

==

Q. Then how do you know that she got it from the defendant?

A. Carlotta's ghost told me.

Q. You were given this information by a ghost?

A. Yes, I was.

Q. Do you have some type of special ability that allows you to speak to ghosts?

A. No.

Q. You're not a medium?

A. No.

Q. Wouldn't it be easier to believe that someone planted the jewellery in the defendant's girlfriend's apartment than for the information to have come from a ghost?

A. I don't know.

Q. You offered other information to the authorities, is that correct?

A. Yes.

==
===

Q. Information concerning the night of the murder?

A. Yes.

Q. And how did you get this information?

A. In dreams.

Q. You dreamt it all up?

A. No, the ghost of Carlotta appeared to me in my sleep and told me how she was murdered.

Q. I see. And if you would...

In this current presentation, Baptiste suddenly comes under the influence of Carlotta's ghost while giving testimony in court on the witness stand. Both her voice and demeanor change drastically in the depiction of the factual event!

A. I was home alone. He said he was going to come by and do me a favour - fix my television set for me.

—---

Q. Ms. Escobar, are you all right? Do you need to take a break?

A. Then he came in. The defendant. He didn't come to help me, to fix my television. He...he wanted me. And I told him to get out!

Q. Ms. Escobar...

A. He wouldn't leave. Instead he started to chase me. I was terrified! He leapt over the furniture after me like a madman. He grabbed me and yanked me and tossed me around. Then he put his hands around my neck and dragged me over to the sink.

Q. Please, Ms. Escobar!

A. And he shook me and shook me and beat my head against the sink until I was dead.

DEFENSE ATTORNEY TO THE JUDGE

17. Your honor I object to this entire form of testimony. The witness is not speaking under her own volition.

JUDGE TO THE COURT

1. Yes, these proceedings are out of order. I declare a recess until ten a.m. tomorrow morning. I would like to see both counselors in my chambers.

Great legal confusion was caused by the ghostly testimony. When court was convened, the judge would not allow proceedings to continue, declaring that the jury's objectivity had been compromised by the impromptu testimony by the murder victim's ghost.

· **OFFICIAL VERDICT:** *a mistrial was ordered by the presiding judge, meaning that the proceedings had been so corrupted*

==

by unorthodox developments that he did not believe the jury could reach an impartial decision. A new jury would have to be chosen and another trial begun from the beginning.

This was not the end of the matter, however. There was one very important person in the court who was powerfully affected by the ghostly testimony - the

defendant! The description of the murder was so detailed and was such an exact narrative of what had taken place that the murderer was driven to confess.
The murderer was ultimately given the lenient sentence of fourteen years in prison.

A shoemaker's wife was found murdered in her apartment. There were not any witnesses or clues and the husband claimed that he had not been home all night. The police resorted to extreme, unorthodox measures to find the murderer.

· **POINT OF SIGNIFICANCE:** *the method for discovery of the culprit was unique in the annals of ghost hunting, involving transforming by hypnosis a regular person into a telepathic medium with direct contact with supernatural forces.*

The wife of a shoemaker was found dead in her bed in the couple's apartment in Bernburg, Germany. There wasn't any incriminating evidence and there were not any witnesses. The husband was taken in for questioning, despite his insistence of innocence. He was ultimately released for lack of evidence.

The investigation was at a dead-end. Yet, a murder had been committed and a murderer had evaded justice.

The police commissioner of this district who was in charge of the investigation undertook desperate measures. He had previously worked with a hypnotist and his partner with whom the commissioner had had success in solving a similar crime.

The hypnotist would place his subject in a deep trance and artificially induce a condition of telepathic sensitivity. With the assistance of supernatural forces, the subject had access to information beyond normal human understanding.

The hypnotist and his subject met the police commissioner at the murder scene. Only the three were on hand.

The hypnotist placed his subject under a trance. In this condition the subject walked around the apartment and, under supernatural direction, picked up and did a "reading" of various objects. In this way, he developed a picture of the events of the night of the murder.

There was a violent argument between the shoemaker and his wife. The woman was beaten into unconsciousness and was flung bodily into the bed. The husband departed, and the wife was still alive when he left. However, the woman had settled in the bed in such an awkward position that her head hung forward, and constricted her windpipe so that she eventually died of suffocation.

When the hypnotised man was finished and revived from his trance he and the hypnotist were asked to leave the premises for a short while. Even though the description given by the "medium" was compelling, a test had to be made of his abilities.

The police commissioner summoned a group of officers into the apartment and had them re-arrange the furniture around the murder scene. He then brought the hypnotist and his subject back into the apartment.

"I want you to tell us how this room looked on the night of the murder," the commissioner told them. "Point out what piece of furniture should go where and I'll have my men move it."

The hypnotist placed his subject under a trance again and they set about re-arranging the décor. While this took place, the commissioner compared the emerging setting to the one of the murder night which he'd sketched on a notepad and was now holding before him.

The outcome was a perfect match!

Armed with this information, the police commissioner brought the husband back to headquarters for questioning. The commissioner described in step-by-step fashion details of how the murder was committed.

As in the case of the murdered Philippine nurse, the murderer was so overcome by the accuracy of the depiction of the crime

==

and was so distraught by guilt that he confessed.

· **OFFICIAL VERDICT:** *the husband was convicted of manslaughter in the first degree.*

DOCKET # 6A (1922) MURDER OF ERIC TOMBE, SURREY, ENGLAND

Eric Tombe purchased part ownership in a racing stable. For unknown reasons he was murdered by his partner. His body was secretly disposed of and the location was finally disclosed by the deceased's ghost appearing in a series of dreams to his mother.

· **POINT OF SIGNIFICANCE:** *the deceased's mother could not have known of the location of her son's body except by supernatural means because neither she nor her husband knew about their son's interest in the racing stable where he was buried. The parents did not even know that their son had been killed.*

The mother of Eric Tombe began

experiencing horrific nightmares. Night after night they assailed her. Night after night, she relived the terror of seeing her son shot to death then hastily disposed of. But these were more than mere dreams. These were genuine contacts by the spirit of the deceased son by interjecting himself into the realm of sleep.

This is a fascinating aspect of the supernatural that receives little

OOOOOOOOOOOOOOOOOOOOOOOOOOOOOOOOOOOOOOOOOOOOOOOOOOOOOOOOOOOOOOOO

attention. These are not JUST dreams. They are genuine contacts with a conscious force from another realm.

Neither Mrs. Tombe, nor her husband Gordon - who was a parson - were aware of the existence of the racing stables of which their son had become a part owner. Since they were not fans of horse racing, the locations of racing stables was not in their general sphere of knowledge. Yet - night after night - Mrs. Tombe was psychically taken to a particular racing stable guided by her son.

Mrs. Tombe implored her husband to conduct a search for the location of the stable appearing in her night terrors. Unfortunately, it's precise location was never divulged in the dreams - just a specific stable somewhere in the countryside.

In order to placate his wife, the parson consulted various realty firms and studied a variety of sporting magazines that catered to the racing fan. The Reverend was startled to find a photograph and accompanying literature about a racing stable that exactly matched his wife's description. It was in Surrey, England.

The parson sought out the authorities there and - in deference to his position in the church - they undertook a search of the designated area. According to Mrs. Tombe, her son had been dumped into a damp, cramped underground pit of some type.

The police found four cesspits on the stable grounds. They undertook the gruesome, strenuous search for the young Eric Tombe's body, having to raise the ponderous, concrete slabs that overlay the cesspits. Within one of the pits was the partially decomposed body of Eric Tombe, a section of his head having been blown off by a gunshot.

There weren't any leads as to who the murderer was. But as in so many of these types of cases, it was the killer's own guilt which eventually did him in.

In a completely unrelated incident the police were walking up to the apartment of a man who was wanted for writing and cashing bad checks. His name was Ernest Dyer. He was a former part owner of a racing stable in Surrey, England. He was also the guilt-ridden murderer of Eric Tombe.

Ernest Dyer would not let them take him alive. He took out his gun - probably the same one he'd used to kill Eric Tombe

- placed it to his own head, pulled the trigger, and blew out his own brains.

· **OFFICIAL VERDICT:** *Ernest Dyer was suspected of the murder of Eric Tombe but the crime remained unsolved without any other suspects.*

On or about April 14th in the year 1690 William Barwick murdered his pregnant wife. On April 22nd of that same year the ghost of the murdered woman appeared to her brother-in-law Thomas Lofthouse

==

and revealed to him the location of her hastily buried body and the identity of the person who had killed her.

· **POINT OF SIGNIFICANCE:** *No one was even aware of the crime until the ghost made her presence known to her brother-in-law and at the same time revealed the location of her body.*

This is a quaint ghost story, if perhaps in a morbid way. Quaint in that it is in reality an old-fashioned ghost story with a moral and a just ending.

For reasons never fully understood, William Barwick killed his pregnant wife. Shortly after the deed he appeared at the home of Thomas Lofthouse - brother-in-law of the deceased woman - and told him that he'd sent his wife to stay with

his uncle Harrison in Selby. He said that she would receive better attention at his uncle's house.

That was on April fourteenth. Eight days later - on April 22nd - Mr. Lofthouse was visited by the ghost of the deceased woman. It wasn't a spectacular, frightening or - at the outset - even a noteworthy visitation, simply an unexpected appearance. He wasn't even

sure she was a ghost at first because the woman whom he had seen near his yard had simply gone away abruptly and may have merely walked off when he wasn't looking. This turned out not to be the case.

Mr. Lofthouse immediately told his wife about the odd occurrence. She was greatly distressed and, fearing for her sister, insisted that her husband pay a visit to William Barwick's uncle as soon as possible. He did so the next day. Harrison told him that Mrs. Barwick had not been brought to his home to be taken care of by his nephew or anyone else and that this news made him fear for her well being.

On April 23rd Thomas Lofthouse paid a visit to the Mayor of York. In his offices he executed a deposition in which he described the particulars of what he knew about the missing Mrs. Barwick.

On the 24rth, William Barwick also visited the Mayor's office. He confessed to the crime of murdering his wife and was placed in jail to await what seemingly would be a quick trial. The date was set for September seventeenth.

Barwick's conviction would not be automatic. As the trial began, he withdrew his confession and entered a not guilty plea.

This set the stage for Thomas Lofthouse to take the stand and describe under oath how he had seen the ghost of the murdered woman not long after her demise. Following is an enactment of his testimony with all of the facts intact.

BY THE PROSECUTOR:

Q. State your name please.
A. Thomas Lofthouse.
Q. Where do you reside, Mr. Lofthouse?
A. In the town of York.
Q. You are the brother-in-law of the deceased?
A. I am.
Q. How did you first learn of Mrs. Barwick's misfortune?
A. I was told by her husband.

Q. He told you that he murdered his wife?
A. No. What I mean to say is that he told me that he had removed her to his uncle's home to be taken care of.
Q. I see. Why didn't you believe this was true?
A. At first, I guess I did. But then I saw an apparition in my garden my viewpoint changed.
Q. An apparition? Of who?
A. My sister-in-law.
Q. You mean Mrs. Barwick?
A. Yes.
Q. Describe the apparition please.
A. It happened while I was watering my quickset hedge during the mid-day on the 22nd of April last.
Q. Go on.
A. Well, there's a public pool outside my back yard and I was taking water from it

to my hedge. On one occasion as I was walking down the path to refill my bucket I found myself walking behind a young woman.

Q. did you recognise her?

A. Not at first. I only saw her from the back. She continued off the path to the right where there's a bench. The woman took a seat there while I continued past her.

Q. Was there anyone else around at the time?

A. No just she and I.

Q. Go on. What happened next?

A. I filled my bucket with water at the edge of the pool and started back toward my yard. As I did I passed the woman again who was still in the bench dandling something in her lap.

Q. Then what?

A. I took the bucket to my hedges and poured the water on them. Then I turned from my yard to look toward the pool. The woman was gone.

Q. Why did you assume that this woman was your sister-in-law?

A. I got a better look at her on my way back to the hedge with the filled bucket. She wore the same brown dress and white hood as my sister-in-law commonly wore.

Q. Did you speak to her at any time?

A. No.

Q. Why not?

A. Like I said - at first I wasn't really sure who she was. Then when I recognised her I was surprised to see my sister-in-law and wondered why she hadn't spoken to me. I was going to talk to her, but she'd disappeared.

Q. Are you aware that William Barwick formerly admitted to murdering her and then withdrew his confession?

A. Yes. But he had to have killed her. He knew where her body was.

Q. You were the one who discovered the body, correct?

A. Yes. I assumed that the ghost had appeared where she did because that was the spot where Barwick must have buried her. So, with my wife and a friend looking on, I dug in that spot and found the body still wearing the same clothes I saw her dressed in when she appeared to me.

Q. And that is the conclusive evidence that must convict William Barwick. Because in his confession - before you recovered the body - William Barwick claimed to having drowned the victim in that very pond and then buryied her hard by. How could he possibly have known she was buried there if he hadn't been the one who buried her?

A. And my sister-in-law's ghost showed me exactly where she was buried.

· **OFFICIAL VERDICT:** *William Barwick was found guilty of murder in the first degree and was sentenced to be hung by the neck until dead bound in chains. The sentence was duly carried out.*

DOCKET # 8A STATE VS KING NY TIMES 10-10-21

A seventeen-year-old high school student named Arline Stout was found dead in her living room. Suicide was at first suspected, but on additional information supplied by the deceased's ghost murder charges were brought against her boyfriend.

· **POINT OF SIGNIFICANCE:** *without the ghostly evidence the death of Arline Stout would have remained classified as a suicide.*

Arline's father came home one afternoon to find his daughter lying dead on the living room sofa attired in a nightdress. She had suffered a bullet wound to her right shoulder, a wound that caused her death. At the girl's side was an empty Army revolver which had been kept by

---

her father in a desk drawer in the hallway. It was now missing one cartridge.

The official cause of death was listed as suicide. There was not any evidence pointing toward foul play. There were not any witnesses to the shooting. Suicide seemed to be the only reasonable explanation.

Arline's father was distraught. He certainly had to blame himself for her death, having left his revolver within easy reach of anyone who should wish to use it. But could he ever have expected his daughter to take her own life!

A few days after Arline's funeral, her inconsolable father visited her gravesite. It was a quiet day in mid October. No one else was around. He desperately wanted to be near his daughter.

As the grieving man stood looking over her grave, eyes set in the near distance on nothing in specific - a remarkable vision appeared before him. The form of his deceased daughter appeared to him directly across her own grave.

She then spoke to him, her words coming as if a crinkling of the autumn leaves in the wind. Arline told him, in effect, "I did not kill myself." This is what her father later told police.

After her first unclear remarks, her next words were very clearly heard by her father. "Father, go to see Edwin. He can tell you all."

Arline's ghost then vanished. Her stunned father remained staring into the emptiness she'd left, trying to make sense of what he'd just seen and heard. It took Mr. Stout a couple of days to regain his composure. He decided to tell the police a story that he wasn't sure they'd believe.

Arline's father went to the police station and made this verbatim report: "I went to my daughter's grave on Saturday. While I stood there a vision appeared over the grave and Arline stood there. 'Father,' she told me, 'go to see Edwin. He can tell you all.'"

His daughter's ghost also told him that she had visited Edwin herself in an attempt to convince him to confess to the crime but that he would not do so.

The Edwin spoken of by the ghost was twenty-one-year-old Charles Edwin King the late girl's most recent boyfriend.

The police had already questioned King who had declared his innocence. He said that the last time he'd seen Arline was the afternoon before her death, and he had spent the rest of the day in the nearby town of Bristol.

According to King, it would not have been possible for him to have made the journey back to Arline's house from Bristol in the timeframe required for him to have murdered her. Originally, the police agreed with this assessment. King further told the authorities that he was still in Bristol when he heard of Arline's death.

Armed with the graveside evidence given them by Arline's father, the police now had reason to delve deeper into King's story. They quickly discovered that there wasn't anyone in Bristol who could account for the young man's whereabouts during the critical time when Arline was shot.

Even more damaging was that witnesses unavailable previously had become available, witnesses whom King said would verify his presence. They didn't. Thus, not only could no one be found who could substantiate King's presence in Bristol the people whom he had relied on for an alibi did not provide King with this needed confirmation of his whereabouts. This led to King's arrest on suspicion of murder. He was eventually tried and convicted for the slaying of Arline Stout.

· **OFFICIAL VERDICT:** *Charles Edwin King was found guilty of first degree manslaughter.*

DOCKET #9A (1631) THE MURDER OF ANNE WALKER
"The History of Durham"

Anne Walker was the cousin of John Walker and had become pregnant by him. She was sent away by her cousin to a boarding house for wayward women but a short time later was kidnapped and murdered.

· **POINT OF SIGNIFICANCE:** *the angry ghost of the murdered woman appeared on several occasions to an unwilling witness who finally helped bring the guilty pair to trail. The trial that ensued was a sensational one in which supernatural powers took control of events in the most blatant display of paranormal activity in open court to date!*

Anne Walker lived with her cousin and lover John Walker in the village of Great Lumley where there was much gossip about their relationship. Not only did Anne perform the housework for her cousin but she performed more intimate tasks as well, resulting in her becoming pregnant by him.

To quiet the scandalmongers John Walker dispatched his cousin to a boarding house for wayward girls in the nearby town of Chester-Le-Street. The home was run by a woman named Dame Carr. She was reputed to be a warm and caring person. Several days after Anne had been sent to the boarding house a friend of John Walker's named Mark Sharp - a collier (coal-miner) by trade - mysteriously appeared at the door of the home for distressed ladies. Sharp told Mrs. Carr that he'd come to take Anne back home to her cousin who'd had a change of heart and wanted to care for the girl himself.

Dame Carr was suspicious but she had to tell Anne the news. Anne was delighted. She hurriedly packed her belongings and rushed out to join Mark Sharp who was waiting for her in his coach. Anne was driven away and never seen alive again.

Her ghost, however, became quite active. And she had one primary target of visitation - a mill owner named James Graime.

As is very common in these situations the ghost of the murder victim approaches a complete stranger to seek assistance. Neither friend, lover, relative nor representative of the authorities would be contacted - but a complete stranger.

Why this is so in cases of a ghost seeking help isn't clear. It's possible that the psychic self of the deceased person is still in a state of shock and simply contacts the first person that the spirit comes across.

Or perhaps there is some occult law of psychic attachment that causes the ghost to be drawn to a particular psyche.

There isn't any reason known as yet why the ghost of a distressed soul contacts one person rather than another.

In any event, James Graime certainly did not wish to be contacted by the ghost of Anne Walker, judging by his lack of response. It wasn't until her third visitation of him that Mr. Graime did the bidding of the ghost which was to contact authorities and have her story made public.

It was to placate the spirit of Anne walker that James Graime walked into the Magistrate's office on December 21, 1630 and provided his deposition. What follows is an enactment of what occurred that day with all of the statements true and the facts intact as presented to the Magistrate.

BY THE MAGISTRATE

Q. State your name for the record.

A. James Graime.

Q. How are you employed?

A. I am the owner of a grinding mill.

Q. You are here today to reveal for the record the visitations you have had with the ghost of a young woman named Anne walker.

A. Yes.

Q. When was the first visitation?

A. About a fortnight ago.

Q. Why has it taken you this long to come forward?

A. I didn't think I'd be believed.

Q. But you are here in court now. Why?

A. The ghost has been railing at me with such vigour to come forward that I'd do anything to have peace from it.

Q. Tell us about the first time you witnessed the ghost of Anne Walker.

A. Like I said - it was about a fortnight ago and I was working alone in my mill. It was about the witching hour and I was just about to pour a bucketful of fresh corn into the hopper when I was affrighted by this horrific sight.

Q. Can you describe what you saw?

A. There was a horribly disfigured woman standing all of a sudden in the middle of the floor.

Q. What do you mean by horribly disfigured?

A. There were five great wounds in her head as if she'd been struck by a pick. Her hair was hanging all around her, stringy and blood soaked. She was nothing of this world.

Q. What did you do?

A. I blessed myself as many times as I could and asked the Lord to protect me.

Q. What happened next?

A. I asked the spirit who she was and why she was there?

Q. Did she reply?

A. Yes. She said that she was the spirit of Anne Walker, who had lived with John Walker. She told me that John Walker promised her that she should be taken to a place to be well cared for and then would come back to his home as usual.

Q. Did she say more?

A. Yes. One night a person named Mark Sharp took her away from Dame Carr's boarding home where she was staying.

Q. Why did he take her away?

A. The spirit said that Sharp took her to a moor nearby and beat her savagely about the head with the type of pick that men use to dig coal. She showed me the wounds in her head, which were already plain to see.

Q. She was murdered by Mark Sharp?

A. Yes. And afterward he threw her body into a deep coal pit hard by where he thought no one would ever find her.

Q. Anything more about that night?

A. Yes. Mark Sharp hid the pick he used to kill her under some rocks in a nearby bank. He tried to wash the blood from his shoes and stockings but they were too soiled so he tried to hide them, too.

Q. And the ghost of Anne Walker came to you to tell you these things?

A. Yes and so that I would tell the authorities.

Q. There's still something that bothers me about what you've told us - how long it took you to first bring this information forward: a fortnight. You said it was because you were afraid you wouldn't be believed. Is there another reason?

A. Yes. I was afraid I'd be accused of the murder.

Q. But you're not afraid of that happening now?

A. No. Because it occurred to me: you have the evidence of who the real killer was. It's there right by Anne's body. Mark Sharp's pick, and his bloodied stockings and shoes. They point directly at him.

This is essentially what James Graime told the authorities. A search was made for Anne Walker's body in the location given by her ghost to Mr. Graime and it was found deeply buried in a coal pit, so deeply that it was unlikely that anyone would simply stumble onto it.

Also found nearby were the blood saturated stockings and shoes belonging to Mark Sharp, as well as the murder weapon.

The case went to trial in August of 1681 and the ghostly activity continued. Many of the written accounts of the proceedings describe a supernatural atmosphere pervading the courtroom. Some people even officially reported seeing ghosts in attendance.

The trial went on irrespective of the occult influence. Among the living witnesses who took the stand was Dame Carr. Her testimony was the most damaging to the defendants. She made positive identification of Mark Sharp as being the person who had taken Anne Walker from her boarding house and thus being the last person to see the distressed woman alive.

And - as noted - while the testimony was ongoing, ghosts were seen in the courtroom. Among the witnesses to these ghosts was none other than the presiding judge. He was stunned by the sight of a wraithlike figure hovering over the shoulder of the defendant Mark Sharp.

So alarmed was the judge that he called a sudden halt to the proceedings and declared court in recess for the day. He did not discuss the matter with anyone and kept secret what he'd seen until after the trial was concluded.

There was at least one other person in the courtroom who saw the same ghost, but from a different perspective. This was the jury foreman, a man named Fairbair. He'd also seen the wraithlike ghost hover over the shoulder of Mark Sharp, and like the judge didn't reveal what he'd seen until after the trial.

Neither the judge nor the foreman knew that the other had seen the same ghost! The foreman considered his sighting of such a momentous nature that afterward he had it placed in the official records of the court proceedings, giving a sworn statement describing the apparition he had seen.

Likewise, the judge also later revealed what he had seen. In a letter to a close friend - a man named Serjeant Hutton - the judge described what he had seen and the chilling effect it had had on him.

News of the sightings was published independently. Both men must have been shocked to discover that another person had seen the same ghost and certainly must have been relieved to learn this information.

How many other people had had the same type of vision but did not report it for various reasons?

The judge and the foreman were wise to keep secret the knowledge of their ghostly sightings until after the trail. Releasing such news before the verdict had been rendered may have had damaging effects to the case of the prosecution.

· **OFFICIAL VERDICT**: *Mark sharp and John Walker were both found guilty by the jury of murder in the first degree of Anne Walker and her unborn child. The judge declared their punishment to be death by hanging until dead. The sentence was duly carried out.*

Extremely important to note is that paramount importance was given to evidence that had been supplied by the ghost of Anne Walker. Otherwise, James Graime might have been considered a logical suspect.

The defence tried to imply that the reason James Graime knew so much about the murder was because he himself had been the murderer. The court chose instead to believe that it was the ghost of Anne

Walker which had supplied him with the critical information.

In addition, James Graime did not have a motive to murder Anne Walker nor is there any proof that he even knew her before meeting her ghost. And there was the indisputable evidence of the bloody shoes and stockings as well as the murder weapon which would not have been discovered if not for ghostly intervention. These articles were proved to have belonged to Mark Sharp.

Anne Walker's ghost wanted her killers to be brought to justice. And they were!

CLOSING STATEMENT

The nine cases that were presented here are extremely rare; that's why there are only nine. Even one such case, however, would have been of astounding import because it would involve the supernatural making direct contact with this world.

These are far more than simply interesting ghost stories. They are the strongest legal proof of the existence of ghosts. People were executed based on evidence supplied by ghosts!

What must be understood is the significance of the admission of evidence into a legal proceeding that has been obtained through ghostly intervention. The very act of admitting such evidence is an affirmation of the existence of ghosts.

When evidence is officially accepted the court is acknowledging that the source which supplied that evidence is a valid, genuine source. SOMETHING THAT DOES NOT EXIST CANNOT OFFER EVIDENCE IN COURT! Evidence can only be supplied by something that has existence in reality. Therefore, after examining these nine cases the verdict of the court can only be: **GHOSTS DO EXIST!**

PART II HAUNTED HOUSES

LEGALLY HAUNTED HOUSES

OPENING STATEMENT

This is the second volume in the three volume treatise entitled: GHOSTS IN COURT. Volume 2 examines the existence of legally haunted houses. The keywords are <u>legally</u> <u>haunted</u>.

The houses to be investigated are not simply any old house that people claimed to be haunted. These are houses that a court or other legally constituted body have adjudged to be legally haunted. Every case is true and is fully documented. Most of the documentation is in the form of official court records.

This is a book about ghosts and true ghost stories and how the legal system has been directly affected by the supernatural. **This is NOT a book about psychic detectives or so-called crime-solving mediums!!**

DOCKET # B1 (1550) BOLACRE VS PIQUET

BOLACRE V PIQUET 1550

Giles Bolacre rented a house in the suburbs of Tours, France from a man named Pierre Piquet. Soon after moving in, noises of a ghostly nature began to disturb the Bolacre family on a nightly basis. Due to these disturbances Mr.

Bolacre petitioned the circuit court to be freed from his lease.

· **POINT OF SIGNIFICANCE:** *Giles Bolacre was successful in his initial suit and the court ruled that his house was indeed made uninhabitable by ghostly manifestations. However, due to his failure to obtain the necessary legal documents known as letters royal, the*

---

finding was overturned on a technicality and a second much more detailed hearing was convened.

Both parties in the appeal secured very able legal representation. The landlord - Pierre Piquet - hired an attorney named Maitre Chopin who had a reputation for being an excellent orator.

Giles Bolacre - the tenant - countered with

an equally renowned orator by the name of Nau.

The original case was heard at the local court in Tours. The appeal came before the Cour de Parlement in Paris.

Since the particulars of the case were clear - Mr. Bolacre and his family heard and were disturbed by ghostly noises and their landlord declared that their claims were little more than poppycock - the

---

proposition factored down to which side could make the other side look the more foolish.

"A noise and routing of invisible spirits suffered neither myself nor my family to enjoy a restful sleep when night time was upon us," said Mr. Bolacre, summing up the entire matter.

During the first trial various witnesses were called who succeeded in convincing

the court that the house was haunted and that Giles Bolacre should be freed from his lease. The verdict is the only record of that first case.

The appeal that followed was basically an argument between the attorneys. Since this was an appeal the addition of new evidence would not be expected.

Mr. Chopin, the attorney for the landlord, stepped up first. (Note: the wording to follow is not exact, however the facts as presented are true in every detail)

BY CHOPIN:

As the court is aware, the judge at Themis in the Province of Tours has set down the ruling that the house in question is infested with noisy spirits resulting in a haunting which is an insupportable nuisance. On these grounds he issued an order which effectively voided the lease between the two parties involved.

PRESIDING JUDGE

Yes, and your clients have filed this appeal on the technical argument that the judge in Tours did so without issuing the proper letters royal.

BY CHOPIN

Indeed so. And it was a highly glaring omission by someone in such a responsible office. It was an especially embarrassing blunder when taking into account that a minor, Nicolas Macquereau - for whom Mr. Piquet acts as legal guardian - is involved in these proceedings. By his actions, the judge in Tours has **merely and mischievously** (precise wording highlighted) encouraged the superstition which results in the belief that a house can be haunted.

PRESIDING JUDGE

Aside from that matter, what is your chief contention before us today?

BY CHOPIN

Basically that this entire matter is nothing but foolishness and should not even be before this high body. I would contend that Bolacre and his family suffer from nightmare. They should seek the aid of a physician, not seek the aid of a solicitor to assault my client.

What's more - all ghosts, brownies, and lutins are bugbears of children. I offer such respected great minds as Plato, Empedocles, Marcus Aurelius, Tertullian, Quintillian and Dioscoridies who offer the same advice in their outstanding philosophies.

But, even if it were granted that the Bolacre home is truly haunted by some form of creature belonging to another reality, I would argue that they brought this pestilence with them from wherever they have previously resided.

If not a physician, the Bolacres would be better advised then to seek the assistance of clergy. I wholeheartedly agree with the sage advice given by Alexis Comnenus when speaking of dealing with psychical phenomena - seek the aid of a bishop. It is the tenant's responsibility to have his own bogie exorcised.

But let us assume that the Bolacre home is indeed infested with some form of supernatural bugaboo: this is not reason to void a valid lease! Legally, a valid lease can only be voided in the case of material defect or nuisance of a pestilential air, neither of which are part of this proceeding or have even been considered as such.

With that I close, seeing no legal reason why this lease should be voided and arguing strenuously that the original outrageously erroneous ruling of the judge in Tours be soundly overturned.

Then it was Mr. Nau's turn to present his argument in favour of the tenants.

BY NAU

Honourable members of the court. I sit amused at many of the outrageously erroneous remarks made by my learned colleague. I would ask him by what authority he chastises the judge at Tours when his own knowledge of the words of the very philosophers and wise men he quoted is at best sadly incorrect.

Tertullian, the church father, was certainly a firm believer in the existence of ghosts, ghosts being the spirits

---

released from Purgatory by the Lord to perform acts of contrition within the earthly realm. Yet Mr. Chopin numbers Tertullian among the non-believers. A very amusing stance.

Did Mr. Chopin actually aver that Plato did not believe in spirits? Then I must assume that Mr. Chopin has never read that great work by Plato, *Phaedo*, in which that very subject is well treated.

My learned colleague seems to be implying that the ancient Greeks and Romans scoffed at the existence of ghosts. I'm amazed at such lack of knowledge of the Classical mind and their belief system.

Has Mr. Chopin ever read anything written by Pliny, Plutarch or Suetonius regarding hauntings? Apparently not since hauntings are accepted as

genuine phenomena by the writers just mentioned.

Surely Mr. Chopin is aware that the archfiend Caligula was once ruler of Rome and that the ghost of Caligula was seen by many witnesses to be infesting his former home? Is he also not aware that the authorities of the day chose the most effective way to rid the location of such a diabolical spectre by literally tearing

the building asunder and performing cleansing rituals over the naked ground? I'm certain that neither Mr. Chopin nor Mr. Piquet would like to see that action taken against the house in question in this matter. Indeed, they should be overjoyed that all that is being requested is that the tenants be freed from the lease. The matter before us today remains the same as that which it was previously: the

(error here)

released Giles Bolacre from the obligation of the remainder of his lease. Thus, this house was declared - for a second time - legally haunted.

DOCKET # B2 (1849) LERIBLE VS LE DROIT NEWSPAPER

manifestations which the newspaper the Le Droit claimed were of his own making. Mister Lerible sued the paper for libel.

· **POINT OF SIGNIFICANCE:** *as noted, this is a case of libel. Mister Lerible's house became the target of poltergeist like attacks from the exterior which were witnessed by hundreds of people. A supernatural cause was the only*

Reported by the Gazette Des Tribunaux February 2, 1849

Mister Lerible was a miserly coal merchant who owned a small shack of a house in the centre of a combination coal yard/lumber yard in Paris, France. The house was the object of malevolent spirit

reasonable explanation.

The city of Paris was engaged in a major road building project near Lerible's property. A new byway was being constructed which was to join the Sarbonne to the Pantheon as well as the school of law.
In the middle of the construction zone was a small street known as the Rue Des

BY PLAINTIFF'S ATTORNEY
Q. How is it that you've come by the information you are about to share with us?
A. I am one of the labourers who is building the road to join the Sarbonne to the Pantheon.
Q. What at first made you suspicious about the house in question?
A. Why - there was a great crashing

sound. We all heard it.
Q. Who else do you mean when you say you all heard it?
A. The other workmen.
Q. Describe to the court if you will what you saw and heard.
A. First I heard this loud crashing sound. Something struck the side of the little house. I didn't see what it was but I did see what struck it next. A huge paving stone

- probably at least 100 pounds in weight - bashed into the side of the house.

Q. Where did this paving stone come from?

A. It seemed to come out of nowhere.

Q. Nowhere?

A. At first I thought it might have fallen from the nearby cliff, but realized that that couldn't be.

Q. Why not?

A. Because of the angle at which it struck the wall. To hit the wall where it did, the paving stone would've had to have fallen straight down from above, stopping in mid air, make a right angle turn, and then start flying again toward the house. Such a move is impossible.

Q. You're sure of what you saw?

A. Yes.

ERROR HERE

Q. How is it that you've come by the information you are about to share with us?

A. I am one of the labourers who is building the road to join the Sarbonne to the Pantheon.

Q. What at first made you suspicious about the house in question?

A. Why - there was a great crashing sound. We all heard it.

Q. Who else do you mean when you say you all heard it?

A. The other workmen.

Q. Describe to the court if you will what you saw and heard.

A. First I heard this loud crashing sound. Something struck the side of the little house. I didn't see what it was but I did see what struck it next. A huge paving stone - probably at least 100 pounds in weight - bashed into the side of the house.

Q. Where did this paving stone come from?

A. It seemed to come out of nowhere.

Q. Nowhere?

A. At first I thought it might have fallen from the nearby cliff, but realized that that couldn't be.

Q. Why not?

A. Because of the angle at which it struck the wall. To hit the wall where it did, the paving stone would've had to have fallen straight down from above, stopping in mid air, make a right angle turn, and then start flying again toward the house. Such a move is impossible.

Q. You're sure of what you saw?

A. Yes.

Q. Is it possible that the paving stone was thrown by someone?

A. I guess it would be possible. But he'd have to have the strength of Hercules. But I didn't see anyone in the vicinity who could've thrown it anyway.

Q. Was Mr. Lerible there? Could he have thrown the paving stone?

A. No. He wasn't there. No one was standing in the direction from which the stone came.

Mister Lerible's attorney was attempting to prove that his client was nowhere in the vicinity from where the objects had come and therefore could not have been responsible for throwing them. The next witness to be examined was a neighbour of Mr. Lerible's - a well known bookseller.

BY PLAINTIFF'S ATTORNEY

Q. How are you acquainted with the plaintiff, Mr. Lerible?

A. I am his neighbour.

Q. Would you classify Mr. Lerible as the type of person who seeks notoriety?

A. Not at all. On the contrary, he is quite reclusive by nature.

Q. To the point of being anti-social would you say?

A. Yes, I would.

Q. Do you often see him out on walks through the neighbourhood?

A. I've never seen him walk through the neighbourhood.

Q. Are you aware of the damage that has been recently done to his house?

A. Yes.

Q. Have you witnessed any of these attacks?

A. Yes.

Q. Can you describe what you saw?

A. A most remarkable sight! It happens around dusk - always around that time - when all type and manner of debris appears from nowhere and flies directly against his house, battering it without mercy.

Q. Did you see anyone throw the debris?

A. No. Like I said, it came out of nowhere.

Q. Can you be more specific about what kind of debris you saw?

A. Certainly. There are bricks, paving stones, nails, chunks of metal of unknown type, rocks, stones, lumber, tree limbs, very large chunks of concrete, boulders, sign posts. I could go on.

Q. No, I think that is enough. Now tell me - did you see anyone at any time throw any of this debris?

A. No, sir.

Q. Did someone maybe attach the debris to a catapult-like device and fling it at the house?

A. No, sir.

Q. Did Mr. Lerible throw any of the debris?

A. Certainly not. Look at the man - frail as a titmouse.

Q. So - where did the debris come from?

A. Completely out of nowhere.

Q. And always at dusk?

A. Always.

Q. Thank you, sir.

The next witness to be examined was probably the most damaging. He was the chief inspector of the local police force.

BY PLAINTIFF'S ATTORNEY

Q. State your occupation please, sir.

A. I am the chief inspector of the police force.

Q. You are familiar with the attacks on the home of Mr. Lerible?

A. Indeed, I am. We have a long record of the times that Mr. Lerible has contacted us for assistance.

Q. Mister Lerible contacted you?

A. Indeed so. I have lost count of the number of times.

Q. Why did he contact you?

A. He wanted us to apprehend whoever was bombarding his house with debris.

Q. Did you ever apprehend anyone?

A. No, sir.

Q. Why not?

A. There was not anyone to apprehend.

Q. Was Mr. Lerible the cause of the bombardment of his home?

A. No, sir.

Q. How can you be so sure of that?

A. Because on several occasions he stood on watch with us as his house was being bombarded.

Q. What do you mean by 'On watch?'

A. I stationed an entire squad of officers on lookout at the vicinity of his house on several occasions when the attacks were underway. We even stood on the cliffs just above his house to get a wide view of the entire area.

Q. And what results did your 'watch' produce?

A. None. As the previous witnesses have all testified to: the bombardment came from thin air.

This was damning evidence against the Le Droit newspaper in its claim that Mr. Lerible was the cause of his own misfortune.

Finally, it was Lerible's turn to testify. He had a great deal to say and all of it very compelling.

These are his EXACT words when interviewed on the matter:

"Would you believe it, that they had the nerve to accuse me of all this - me, the owner, who has been more than thirty times to the police to ask them to deliver me, who on the 29th of January went to the Colonel of the Twenty-fourth who sent me a platoon of his Chasseurs?"

Lerible charged this platoon of Chasseurs with the task of finding who was waging the attack on his home. He challenged them to prove that it was he or if it was a person or persons employed by him. The platoon of soldiers could find no physical being responsible for the bombardment of Lerible's house.

Lerible continued speaking his mind: "And another thing: suppose it was I who demolished myself. Should I have furnished the house specially with new furniture, as I did a month before? Should I have had all my furniture spoilt, like the sideboard with mirrors, which the stones seemed to be aimed at?"

At this point, Lerible was showing someone the wreckage made of the furnishings in his home, describing the wanton destruction. There were fragments of broken crockery, his clock, his flower vases, his mirrors, fragments of things valued at 1,500 francs.

He then pointed out a most stunning sight, not only because of the damage but because of the implication of the conscious intent of the supernatural attacker. It was a room filled with stones and piles of long, flat tiles.

When asked about the long, flat tiles, he replied, "Oh! That is because I had closed my shutters. Look at that slit; it is very long and narrow. Well, sir, no sooner had I closed my shutters than all the stones had the shape which you see, and all came through this slit, which is just about that width."

Thus, Lerible tried to fend off the attack by closing his shutters and the assailing force simply acquired - somehow - long, flat tiles which it propelled through the slit opening that was left available.

The evidence was overwhelming. Lerible certainly was not guilty of perpetrating the attack on himself by himself or with the aid of an accomplice!

- **OFFICIAL VERDICT:** *The Le Droit newspaper was found guilty of libel against Mr. Lerible and was ordered to pay a heavy fine in damages as restitution.*

As a byproduct, the physical substantiality of a poltergeist-like being was proved. There could be no other explanation.

But why did it appear here and why did it appear now? The answer to this is quite clear. The attacks on Lerible's home coincided with the beginning of construction of the new road. Most of the projectiles aimed at his home were some form of building material.

Obviously, a sacred ground had been disturbed by the construction. Elemental spirits were aroused and angered by this trespass and - for reasons still unknown - Lerible's home was at the centre of the supernatural storm that ensued.

A police constable noted in his "occurrence book" that an annoying ghost was appearing nightly at a specific house. The story was picked up by a local newspaper and this story was in turn picked up and enlarged upon by other newspapers. The owner of the haunted property in question filed a libel suit against the originating newspaper, claiming that the negative reporting on his vacant house lowered its property values and made it even more difficult to let.

The matter first went through a lower court which stated the cause was not actionable and that there was no precedent by which to proceed. In other words, reporting a house to be haunted could not be a cause for libel.

The owner of the property chose to appeal the matter and succeeded in having the original verdict overturned.

- **POINT OF SIGNIFICANCE:** *on the question of* <u>hauntedness</u> *both courts ruled that the house in question was legally haunted but each viewed the impact of the condition of being haunted differently. That's the reason why the rulings were different.*

The verbatim account of the police constable's initial report gave an indication of a haunting and it was through the reporter's "digging" for a story that the haunting's particulars became more widely known.

Some have implied that the entire story was simply a matter of a reporter "making up" facts. This does not appear to be the case. This is a matter of a good reporter uncovering facts that might never have come to the fore and then putting them in print.

The story of the haunted house on St. John's Avenue is best begun with a review of the police report **EXACTLY** as it appeared in the constable's "occurrence book." (Canadian Notes & Query, 1907)

"SECOND HOUSE EAST OF MARIE, ON ST. JOHN'S

AVENUE IS BELIEVED BY SOME PEOPLE TO BE

HAUNTED AT NIGHT BETWEEN 11 AND 12 MIDNIGHT.

THERE ARE PARTIES OF MEN HANGING AROUND THIS

HOUSE, ALSO IN THE BASEMENT, AWAITING THE

APPEARANCE OF THE SPOOK. THIS HOUSE IS

AT PRESENT UNOCCUPIED."

What now follows is the original newspaper report **EXACTLY** as it was written after the reporter did some investigating and came up with more information.

A NORTH END GHOST: There is a ghost in the

north end of the city that is causing a lot of

trouble to the inhabitants. His chief haunt is in

a vacant house on St. John's Avenue, near to

Marie. He appears late at night and performs

48

strange antics so that timid people give the place
a wide berth. A number of men have lately made
a stand against ghosts in general and at night
they rendezvous in the basement and close around
the house to await his ghostship, but so far he

still remains at large.

What follows is essentially the argument that was used by the owner of the defamed house in the lower court case as presented by her attorney.

It is clear that the initial story of the haunting was picked up by and greatly

added to by other newspapers. As a result, what started off as a relatively harmless, mildly interesting story has been blown out of proportion into a great tale of fiends and monsters besieging my client's home. This property has been difficult enough for my client to let due to its location - now its value has been even further diminished with the added insinuation of its being haunted.

This type of defamation of a property cannot be allowed to prevail without some manner of remunerative judgment. We are seeking damages from the newspaper which printed the initial story because if this story had not been made public it could not have been disseminated as it was to a much wider audience.

The defence spoke out next and the following is essentially the argument used. Remember, it is the newspaper which is defending itself.

First and foremost, as all of us in this room are aware, the only defence of libel be it against a person or property is truth. And that is our defence. Is there anything within the story written by the employee of my client that is not true? He took his basic facts from an official police department document which was earlier read before this court. We might just as well put the police department on trial here. After all, this is 1907, not the Dark Ages.

The story about the house on St. John's Avenue is news. And as such it comes within the purview of "fair game" as the saying goes.

Now - did the writer of the newspaper article defame the property? Did he say that its walls were rotting and the baseboards were infested with termites? No. Did he say that the ceiling was sagging and about to collapse? Did he say that the basement was overrun with rats? No.

The author of the article wrote about a haunting. Is the house haunted? Yes. It isn't something that the author made up.

It is a fact that he properly reported based upon official police documents and by visiting the scene of the haunting and undertaking interviews as any professional news reporter would.

How can this be libel! Truth is our defence.

Upon listening to the arguments, the judges of the King's Bench of the lower court retired for private deliberation.

Thus, this court denies the request for libel damages. This hearing stands adjourned.

But this did not end the matter. The decision was appealed by the plaintiff - the owner of the house - and the results were different.

The arguments were the same, but the appellate court made a different ruling.

· **FINAL VERDICT ON APPEAL:** *A haunted house by its very nature is worth less than a non-haunted house. As such, when the newspaper that originally published knowledge of the hauntedness of the house to the public did so the value of the house was diminished. If not for the original newspaper article none of the other papers would have printed stories about the haunted house in their*

Both agreed the house had a ghost; they disagreed on what this did to property values and who was liable for disseminating the negative information.

DOCKET # B4 (1885) WALDRON V. KIERNAN

Circuit Court of the City of Dublin, Ireland.

The house of a man named Waldron, which was in the suburbs of Dublin, Ireland came under a ferocious attack of supernatural forces. Despite the overwhelming evidence to the contrary Mr. Waldron insisted on accusing his

---

neighbour, Mr. Kiernan, for the damages caused and sued him in court for relief.

· **POINT OF SIGNIFICANCE:** *There was a plethora of supernatural manifestations connected with this case and there were very many highly credible eyewitnesses to them. That the house was haunted was an undeniable fact.*

Mr. Waldron was a solicitor's clerk and his neighbour Mr. Kiernan was a mate in the merchant's service. For reasons unknown, supernatural forces waged a merciless assault upon the home of Mr. Waldron from August 1884 through January 1885, breaking windows, doors, shutters, and battering the exterior in general.

---

particularly detrimental to her husband's case.

What follows is a presentation of her testimony as it would have appeared with all of the vital details true and intact.

BY THE DEFENCE ATTORNEY
Q. You are Mrs. Waldron, wife of the plaintiff in this case?
A. I am.

Q. Have you observed any of the alleged attacks upon your residence.
A. Of course. I live there.
Q. There was one event in particular that frightened you to the extent that you summoned the local constable to investigate. Do you recall the circumstances of that night.
A. Indeed I do. I was quietly sitting alone in the parlour doing some needlework

when I heard knocking on one of the front windows.

Q. What kind of knocking.

A. Kind? Just a wrapping - like maybe a tree branch hitting the glass.

Q. But it wasn't a tree branch.

A. No.

Q. What did you do.

A. I waited for the wrapping to stop, and when it didn't I got up to see what was causing it.

Q. What did you find.

A. There was a hand at the window. Just a lone hand in mid air on the outside.

Q. Was it Mr. Kiernan's hand?

A. Floating in mid air? No.

Q. What happened next.

A. The hand produced a diamond like cutting edge and started to cut out a hole in the window glass.

Q. You're certain of this.

A. Yes.

Q. What did you do?

A. I watched as the hand finished cutting the hole in the window and then it reached inside. I frantically looked about for some type of weapon and found my husband's tailor's shears nearby.

Q. What did you do with them?

A. I lopped off one of the ghost's fingers is what I did.

Q. What happened to the rest of the hand?

A. After I snipped off the finger the hand drew back out of the window and then vanished.

Q. Did you try to follow the hand - you know, go outside after it?

A. I was too terrified for that. But I did look out the window to make sure it wasn't still lurking near.

Q. Was it?

A. No.

Q. Did you see anyone or anything else outside?

A. No.

Q. Not even Mr. Kiernan?

A. No. He was nowhere in sight.

Q. What did you do after this happened?

A. I summoned the chief constable to my house.

That was the gist of Mrs. Waldron's testimony. Another witness called to the stand was the Waldron's housekeeper. As in the case with Mrs. Waldron, the housekeeper's testimony was more beneficial to Mr. Kiernan's defence. What follows is substantially what the housekeeper said - all of the facts true and intact.

Q. Why do you believe that the house is haunted.

A. Mostly because of the footsteps.

Q. Footsteps.

A. Yes, I often hear footsteps follow me up the stairs as I'm going to the upper rooms.

Q. Is there any other reason you think the house is haunted.

A. I can sense a presence in the house.

Q. What do you mean by presence.

A. Sort of like a feeling of being watched. That there's somebody there but you can't see anybody there.

Q. Do you feel this way often.

A. Whenever I'm in the house.

Q. Records show that you also have summoned the constable to the Waldron house.

A. Yes. Even though the ghost hasn't hurt me it's scared me awfully sometimes.

Q. Do you think it's possible that Mr. Kiernan is the presence you are sensing - that maybe he's hiding in the house somewhere.

A. He'd have to be the best at hiding of anyone who's ever lived.

Q. Do you think he's hiding in the house scaring you.

A. No. Couldn't be him. It's a ghost is what.

Q. Thank you. That'll be all.

The third very damaging witness to Mr. Waldron's case was the chief constable. His testimony is substantially as follows.

BY THE DEFENCE ATTORNEY

Q. You are the chief constable of the district.

A. I am.

Q And you have been called to the Waldron home on several occasions.

A. Yes. There is a stack of reports on my desk dealing with their situation.

Q. Concerning the ghost.

A. The complaints are against Mr. Kiernan.

Q. Not the ghost.

A. There have been many disturbances at the Waldron home and the owner thinks they are caused by Mr. Kiernan so he files a report against him.

Q. Have you investigated these charges.

A. Yes.

Q. What did you find.

A. That there are ongoing attacks made on the Waldron home but none of them can be attributed to Mr. Kiernan.

Q. Are you familiar with the report filed by Mrs. Waldron concerning the spectral hand that cut out a piece of her window pane.

A. Yes I am. I personally investigated.

Q. What did you find.

A. Nothing. There wasn't any glass at all in that one section where the pane would have been.

Q. Can you explain that a little clearer.

A. Well, there weren't any broken edges of glass in the window pane. It was as if that pane simply had had no glass in it at all, not as if someone removed a piece from the centre of it or anything like that.

Q. I see. Did you find any glass splinters or shards of broken glass on either side of the window.

A. Nothing at all. Clean as a hound's tooth as the expression goes.

Q. And what did you deduce from this.

A. The glass had not been broken. This part of the window was simply missing an entire pane of glass. Remember, the full window itself has about six separate lights.

Q. Did you find any sign of the lopped off finger.

A. None at all.

Q. Any blood.

A. No, sir. There wasn't any physical evidence to corroborate Mrs. Waldron's story.

Q. Was there any indication at all that Mr. Kiernan may have been involved in this episode - even if just lurking outside the window.

A. None whatsoever.

Q. But you've told us that you have had previous complaints from Mr. Waldron about Mr. Kiernan.

A. Yes and each one of the complaints was completely unfounded.

Q. Finally - what have your investigations revealed about the part that Mr. Kiernan may have played in these attacks on the Waldron household.

A. There is not the slightest scintilla of evidence pointing toward Mr. Kiernan as being involved in any way whatsoever.

That concluded the chief constable's testimony.

- **OFFICIAL VERDICT:** *Mr. Waldron's statements about Mr. Kiernan being responsible for the attacks made on his home were libellous and he was ordered to pay damages for defaming his name.*

More importantly for this study is that the court also determined the house to be under attack by sinistre undetermined forces. In other words - the house was haunted.

Newly famous English playwright Stephen Phillips rented a cottage in the English countryside with his young daughter and soon found that it was haunted. The haunting was reported in the local newspaper and, because of Mr. Phillips' newfound fame, the newspaper article had a sizeable readership. This caused the owner of the cottage to sue the newspaper for libel because of the bad publicity it produced against his property.

· **POINT OF SIGNIFICANCE:** The haunting became so extreme that the servants decided to leave rather than endure it.

Stephen Phillips was born on July 28, 1864 in Summertown, Oxfordshire, England and was educated at Trinity College, Stratford-Upon-Avon, and King's College. These are very impressive credentials.

Stephen had always had an interest in drama and in 1885, at the age of twenty-one, he began a brief career as an actor with the R.R. Benson Acting Company. Discovering that his true talent lay in writing rather than acting, Mr. Phillips produced his first plays at this time.

It was in 1900 that he wrote his most famous work called *"Paolo and Francesca,"* a shakespearesque romantic drama. In fact, it was so well received that he was favourably compared to THE William Shakespeare.

Paolo and Francesca was a huge commercial success. Mister Phillips made more money with it than he had earned his entire life to date. It allowed him to move out of his cramped and noisy flat in the city and to a quiet place in the countryside where he could write in

Stephen had always had an interest in drama and in 1885, at the age of twenty-one, he began a brief career as an actor with the R.R. Benson Acting Company. Discovering that his true talent lay in writing rather than acting, Mr. Phillips produced his first plays at this time.

It was in 1900 that he wrote his most famous work called *"Paolo and Francesca,"* a shakespearesque romantic drama. In fact, it was so well received that he was favourably compared to THE William Shakespeare.

Paolo and Francesca was a huge commercial success. Mister Phillips made more money with it than he had earned his entire life to date. It allowed him to move out of his cramped and noisy flat in the city and to a quiet place in the countryside where he could write in peace and his daughter could play in the fresh air.

The untimely death of his wife had left his former home with bad memories and it was a very welcome move for he and his daughter. At least in the beginning.

Mister Phillips found what he thought would be a quiet cottage in the countryside and rented it. He was not yet forty-years-old and had hopes of continuing with his successful writing career. His daughter would also hopefully find lots of new playmates. Neither Stephen nor his daughter expected what truly came to pass.

It wasn't long after moving into the cottage that it became clear that something was wrong. It became clear in the strange, sudden reactions of the servants to sounds that came from nowhere. It became clear by the reactions of the family pet which would suddenly howl and growl with terror at some unseen force. It became clear that something unnatural was haunting this house.

The random noises didn't have any pattern or seeming purpose to them. A knock on a bedroom wall. A rapping on a table. A creaking of the stairs when no one was there. The entity did not attempt to communicate with anyone - just make certain that its presence was known by all.

Time and again Mr. Phillips was disturbed from his writing when the study door opened and closed under its own power. The peace that he and his daughter had so desperately longed for was violated on a daily basis.

Even more distressing was what the daughter of Mr. Phillips was seeing. She frequently glimpsed an elf-like creature skittering across the floor and disappearing into a corner. Attempts to track down the elf were made but nothing was ever found.

The appearance of an elfin being was particularly troubling. In parapsychological terms this type of apparition often represents the psyche of a deceased loved one, usually a spouse or a parent.

The figure could either be a genuine spectral appearance in the afterlife of the deceased in this new form or it could be the mental creation of the deceased person by a surviving loved one - an oddly distorted mental image.

In other words, the elf-like being could either have been the late Mrs. Phillips' true astral form projected from the other side or it was the psychic depiction of her that had been developed by the mind of either her former husband or by her daughter. It even could've come from the psyches of both and was commingled into one form.

In any event, it was much more than a mere coincidence that this type of apparition was seen.

The strange noises continued. The study door opened and closed by itself. The elf-like creature continued to race about the house from shadow to shadow.

The servants were first to depart the premises. They could not tolerate the continued terrorisation from the unknown attackers.

Then the Phillips decided that they could no longer stay and they also departed the unquiet house - bitterly disappointed.

This is when the story about the haunting was run in the local newspaper, precipitating the lawsuit for libel.

The court action that came of this was pretty straightforward. Mister Phillips and his daughter were called to testify as to what they had seen. The servants were also put on the stand.

The newspaper waged the standard defence, claiming that the story was true and that printing it was not libelous.

And the court returned with it's usual answer: freedom of speech - be it the truth or not - did have limits. The newspaper went beyond these limits.

· **OFFICIAL VERDICT:** *the court agreed with the landlord that having the house known to be haunted lowered its property values. He was awarded him damages in the amount of 90 pounds. Once again, the ruling meant that the house was legally haunted as well.*

DOCKET # B6 (1835) MOLESWORTH V. WEBSTER
Plaintiff's attorney's notes

Captain Molesworth rented a house from a Mr. Webster who was his next door neighbour in the adjoining building.

After a couple of months residence Mr. Molesworth began being severely disturbed by various types of ghostly noises and assaults.

The captain resorted to literally tearing the house apart around him in search of the ghosts. Not wanting to see his house destroyed, Mr. Webster sought to enforce a cease and desist order against his tenant and then he filed a libel suit against the captain for defaming the reputation of his property.

- **POINT OF SIGNIFICANCE:** *One of Captain Molesworth's young daughters - Matilda - had recently died and many people suspected that the noises were caused by her ghost.*
It was believed that her spirit was trying to contact or warn her invalid sister - Jane -

that she would be joining her shortly in the hereafter.

There are very many witnesses to the events that enfolded in this violently haunted house. The primary facts were taken directly from the notes of Mr. Webster's attorney.

Captain Molesworth moved into the house in May or June of 1835. The location is in an area just outside of Edinburgh, Scotland, known as Trinity. As noted, after a couple of months the household began to be assaulted by a wide variety of noisy and destructive disturbances the source of which Mr. Molesworth went to extremes to locate.

What follows is a representation of Captain Molesworth's remarks on the matter. As always, the statements are true and the facts are intact.

BY PLAINTIFF'S ATTORNEY

Q. You are Captain Molesworth.

A. Yes.

Q. You reside in the house in question.

A. I do.

Q. Tell us something about the disturbances that have been bothering you. Do they occur during the day or the night.

A. Both day and night.

Q. Have you attempted to locate the cause of these disturbances.

A. Of course.

Q. describe to us some of the measures you've taken.

A. At first I tried boring through the wall that connects my house with the landlord's - Mr. Webster's - house. I believed that it was he who was making the noises.

Q. What did you discover.

A. Nothing for certain.

Q. What did you do next.

A. I attacked whatever area the noises came from to see what was making them.

Q. Can you give us an example.

A. There was one time when there was a great pounding from the middle of the parlour wall. So great that you could see the wall throbbing.

Q. What did you do.

A. I attacked it with a pick ax.

Q. With what result.

A. I tore through the wall and down to the boards in the middle. I didn't find anything there.

Q. Can you give us another example.

A. A violent rustling came from the wainscotting. I pried it loose with a hooked bar but didn't find anything. But the noises stopped.

Q. Can you give any more examples.

A. Dozens more. Another time there came a thunderous thumping from the bedroom floorboards. The floor rose and fell like it was about to burst apart.

Q. What did you do.

A. I tore up the floorboards.

Q. Did you find anything.

A. No. But the noises did stop.

Q. Is it true that you even communicated with the ghost.

A. Yes, indeed. It has a consciousness and can communicate.

Q. How did you learn this.

A. One time I was in the dining room with some friends and the noises started just after we finished dinner. I just off hand blurted out to the ghost something like: do you know how many people you're disturbing by this racket.

Q. And the ghost knew.

A. To the number. It rapped out the number of people who were there.

Q. Did you ever try this experiment again.

A. Many times. The ghost always rapped out the correct number.

These essentially were the main points of Captain Molesworth's testimony.

Captain Molesworth was an old soldier who was in a battle with supernatural forces. As an old soldier he sought the help of his old comrades in arms. He brought them to his house and basically had them guard against the unwonted spectral attacks.

Many of the soldiers were later called to the stand, and what follows is a representation of the testimony of one of them with all of the facts intact.

BY THE DEFENCE ATTORNEY

Q. You are a member of the regiment of soldiers who Captain Molesworth asked for help.

A. I am.

Q. Can you tell us about one of the times you tried to track down the ghost in which you were personally involved.

A. Certainly. One time we thought that the ghost might have been outside of the house so we formed a cordon around the house.

Q. That must've taken a lot of men.

A. Yes. But we set up a strong barrier.

Q. Did you catch anything - I guess catch is the best term.

A. No. We didn't get anything.

Q. What else can you tell us about how you tried to help fend of these attacks.

A. There came a time when the investigators thought that maybe the Captain's invalid daughter was somehow to blame for the goings on.

Q. And what happened.

A. Several of us stood on guard around the building - both inside and out - just to be sure, while the girl was tied up about the wrists and ankles and then wrapped tight in a linen bag.

Q. This poor little girl was tied up and confined in bag.

A. It was all very humane, you know. We kept close watch of her.

Q. How long was she kept bound up like that.

A. I don't know that she was particularly bound up.

Q. How long a period was she kept in this unpleasant condition.

A. Until the disturbances resumed again and we could be sure that she wasn't the cause.

Q. How long a time was that.

A. No more than a couple of hours.

Q. Was the cause of the disturbances determined.

A. Not as far as I know.

Q. Never.

A. Never.

This case proceeded through the courts for approximately two years, long after the disturbances suddenly stopped and after Captain Molesworth had vacated the property.

- **OFFICIAL VERDICT:** *Captain Molesworth was ordered to pay restitution for the damage he had done to the property while searching for the noisy ghost. However, the libel suit was dismissed because Mr. Webster did not have any difficulty letting the property to new tenants. Thus, the reputation of the property had not been tarnished by the stories of ghosts.*

DOCKET # B7 (1890) DROGHEDA, IRELAND
F.G. LEE *"Sights and Shadows"*

A family experienced a night of horror due to an attack of supernatural nature. They were legally advised not to pay any more rent. They followed this advice and were sued by the landlady for an entire quarter's rent to be paid immediately.

· **POINT OF SIGNIFICANCE:** *The ghostly assault on the people in this house was particularly violent, including the cause of one very serious injury. Although there were many witnesses to the attack, the judge did not allow any to testify. There appeared to be a great deal of collusion between the judge and the landlady in the final verdict.*

The disturbance began one night at bedtime. Since the husband had been on the scene at each point of attack the descriptions of events will be told as through his testimony. All evidence is factual and intact. The defence attorney represents the tenants.

BY THE PLAINTIFF'S ATTORNEY
Q. To the best of your recollection when did the events of the night in question begin.
A. At bedtime. At least it started at bedtime for my wife and myself. Our children were already asleep.
Q. What was the first occurrence as best as you can recall.
A. Just as my wife and I were about to retire, a foot appeared out of nowhere and kicked the candlestick right off the stand.
Q. Jus a foot.

A. Yes. A disembodied foot.

Q. Then what happened.

A. The entire room lit up as bright as day. The shutters were closed.

Q. Did anything else happen.

A. A ghost appeared near the door dressed in a flowing white gown.

Q. A ghost.

A. Yes, she had something in her hand. I'm not quite sure what it was that she was carrying.

Q. Why is this important.

A. She threw it at my wife and hit her very hard in the chest with it. Then the ghost vanished.

Q. What happened next.

A. Very loud noises came from the room overheard - where our two children and their nurse were. It sounded like the room was being torn apart.

Q. What did you do.

A. I ran upstairs as fast as I could.

Q. What did you see.

A. It was horrible. I couldn't believe it. The floor was all torn up. The furniture was broken. My children were naked and lying senseless in their beds looking like they'd been savagely beaten.

Q. Was there any sign of a ghost in the room.

A. Not at that time. But something had certainly torn apart the room and sorely abused my children.

Q. Then what.

A. I took up both my children in my arms and was leaving the room when it occurred to me: where was the nurse! She was nowhere in sight.

Q. Did you later discover what became of the nurse.

A. Yes. She'd already fled to her mother's house which was not too far away.

Q. What was her condition.

A. Badly beaten and hysterical.

Q. Do you think it possible that she had been responsible for the disturbance that destroyed the upper bedroom and left your children in such a battered state.

A. I can't imagine how that could be possible. Besides, she was just as battered and bruised.

This details the events of that horrific night. Taking the advice of their attorney, the tenants refused to pay any more rent. As already noted, the landlady tried to levy a quarters' rent to be due immediately. When the tenants refused to make the payment, the landlady sued them.

· **OFFICIAL VERDICT BY JUDGE KISBY:** *Since no other witnesses were allowed on the stand to corroborate the tenant's testimony the judge ruled against him and ordered that payment as demanded by the landlady be made.*

Again, collusion between the judge and the landlady seemed highly probable and the spooks in this haunted house outside of Dublin continued their activity as they had done in the past. There were other similar cases brought against this house, but this was the only one – even though with scant details – that was ever recorded.

A car lot where used automobiles were sold came under severe assault from unnatural forces on the morning of September 9, 1960. Arrested and placed on trial was a former employee.

· **POINT OF SIGNIFICANCE:** *Although the location of the haunting is not a house, the infestation falls within the same parameters as those for a haunted house. It is a place that is troubled by supernatural forces.*

The attack began suddenly at 9:30 in the morning and ended as suddenly at 4:30 pm of the same day. A 9 to 5 type of ghost? There's a reason for this, as will be seen.

A hail of stones of differing types and description swept through the car lot as if on a whirlwind. But it wasn't a wind of any natural type that propelled these objects. They were hurled by a supernatural force of unknown origin.

Important to note is that the projectiles did not drop straight downward from above but flew on horizontal paths through the car lot, peppering the automobiles from a sideways direction. Also, there was a three minute interval between storms. Coffee breaks for the ghost?

The manager of the car lot summoned the police. They were baffled when they came on the scene. Their best supposition was that someone from outside of the car lot was using some type of catapult device to fling the stones onto the lot.

Thus, their initial plan was to sweep the surrounding neighbourhood with a search party. Eighteen police officers were called onto the scene and undertook the search.

An additional police officer was stationed atop a nearby tower with a pair of binoculars and a two-way radio. While the search of the neighbourhood did not turn up the culprit, the officer in the tower sighted something very interesting taking place in the parking lot below.

What follows is a representation of his testimony on the matter.

BY THE DEFENCE ATTORNEY

Q. You were among one of the first officers on the scene.

A. Actually, I was stationed atop a billboard that overlooked the auto lot.

Q. Right. You were to keep watch over the entire area.

A. Correct.

Q. And you noticed some unusual activity on the car lot.

A. Yes. I saw a young man leave the manager's office. He seemed angry for some reason.

Q. You could tell that from so far away.

A. Sorry, I was looking through binoculars.

Q. Okay, and did this young man do anything that displayed his anger.

A. Yes, as he was walking through the lot he picked up one of the rocks that had fallen and bashed it against the side of one of the cars.

Q. You saw this.

A. Yes.

Q. Did you see him throw the stone.

A. No.

Q. Did you at any time see him throw any stone.

A. No, sir.

Q. But you did see him pick up a rock and strike a car with it.

A. Yes.

Q. With the rock still in his hand.

A. Yes.

Q. What did you do.

A. I radioed below to one of the officers on the scene and requested that he take the suspect in custody.

Q. And that is how the defendant came to be on trial here today.

A. Yes.

Another person called to the stand was the officer who placed the defendant under arrest. What follows is a representation of his testimony.

BY THE DEFENCE ATTORNEY

Q. You are the arresting officer.

A. Yes.

Q. I'll ask you the same question I asked the other officer: did you at any time see the defendant throw - throw - a rock at any of the automobiles on the lot.

A. No, I did not. The only thing I saw was him striking the side of one of the cars with a rock in his hand.

Q. Are you aware that while the defendant was in handcuffs and being led from

---

the area he was struck by one of these projectiles flying through the auto lot.

A. Yes, I saw him being struck by it.

Q. Can you possibly explain to me how a person in handcuffs can be guilty of hurling a stone across a lot full of cars and striking himself.

A. It would seem impossible.

Q. I'm confused then - why did you arrest him.

A. For interfering with a police investigation.

Q. Not for causing the hail of stones that pelted the auto lot.

A. No, sir. We assumed he hand an accomplice in this.

It was pretty much at this point that the judge intervened and had some pointed questions of his own for the police officer.

What follows is in substance what the judge said.

JUDGE TO POLICE OFFICER

Q. Let me understand something here: the defendant was actually arrested for interfering with a police investigation.

A. Yes, sir.

Q. As I understood the charges, he was considered part of a group of unknown individuals who had unleashed this attack on the auto lot.

A. Originally. That theory has since been abandoned. There were not any other accomplices located, nor was there any type of catapult ever discovered.

Q. The defendant was incarcerated, correct.

A. Yes, sir.

Q. What time approximately was he arrested.

A. Late morning.

Q. And the attacks continued on the auto lot while he was behind bars.

A. Yes, sir.

Q. Then the substance of the district attorney's case escapes me.

A. It is a bewildering case, your honour.

Q. More than that, it's completely without merit. Can you show any other cause for continuing these proceedings.

A. Well, the defendant had once been an employee of this car lot and has fostered ill will against the owner.

Q. What is the cause of the ill will.

A. The defendant worked at a very menial position for which he was paid excessively low wages. This has caused him to hold a grudge against his employer.

Q. Then it would seem the defendant's recourse should be with the Department of Labour.

A. But this isn't an action brought by the defendant.

Q. Once again we are straying far off the subject. What cause of action can you bring against the defendant that links him directly to the attacks made against the car lot.

A. There is nothing I can add to the current charges.

Q. Then your action remains without merit.

This was a case of a true haunting for a day. A seemingly well orchestrated hailstorm of stones and other small projectiles was unleashed on this used car lot on September 9, 1960 between the hours of 9:30 am and 4:30 pm. The time period of the fall of stones completely coincided with a normal workday here - INCLUDING COFFE BREAKS (recall the 3 minute intervals of peace)!

The judge's final remarks are noteworthy. The words in quotations are his.

· **OFFICIAL VERDICT:** *The used auto lot on the day in question came under a blistering attack by "cosmic forces" and can only be attributable to a supernatural agency. All charges against the defendant are dismissed.*

DOCKET # B9 (1991) Nyack, NY
STAMBOVSKY V. ACKLEY
169 A.D. 2d 254

When Mr. Stambovsky discovered that a malevolent spirit occupied his home he sued to have the sale voided due to its hauntedness.

Jeffrey Stambovsky purchased a home from Helen Ackley who did not directly inform him that the house was haunted.

· **POINT OF SIGNIFICANCE:** *This is the penultimate of all haunted house cases - a true classic. The wording of the court's findings literally declared the house "legally haunted" and leaves not a*

---

scintilla of doubt as to the final ruling at law.

Anyone who has ever purchased a house knows the formidable dilemma that an unhappy buyer faces. Once a sale is complete - all the papers are signed, the deeds registered, the document stamps filed, the commissions doled out, and the escrows for taxes and insurance finalised - it is murderously difficult if not absolutely impossible to have all of these transactions voided and/or reversed.

Once the sale of a house is finalised THAT IS THE END OF IT! The new owner owns the house and all of the hidden problems that have come with it.

But what if the problem is a ghost? Not a simple, friendly ghost but a noisy, destructive and terrifying ghost. What to do then!

Jeffrey Stambovsky purchased a Victorian mansion in Nyack, New York from Helen V. Ackley for $650,000. He and his family had been residents of New York City and were seeking the comparatively quiet atmosphere of Nyack. They instead found themselves imprisoned in a house haunted by an angry ghost, stranded far from the people they knew who could help or at least solace them.

Mister Stambovsky finally decided that his only recourse was to take the tortuous route of suing to have the sale of the house vacated.

Real names are used because the proceedings are public record. Important additional information was acquired by this author's personal interviews with several of the primary participants, including the former homeowner and the real estate agent who sold the house.

The additional information is important because the official records do not show the type and the scope of the haunting or the effect it had had on the new owners who were also new parents at the time.

The spectre that stalked this house was not simply noisy but it was loud and obnoxious and seemed intent on driving out the new owners. Cherished keepsakes were broken, everyday items were misplaced to cause frustration and a shady, frightening figure delighted in terrifying the young one occupying the nursery.

The seller's viewpoint deserves noting. Admitting that the ghost existed, Ms. Ackley stated that she never found the spirit to be threatening or violent and that the sense of alarm was caused by the Stambovsky's overactive imaginations. Thus, there were two sides seeing the problem very differently.

The urgent question before the court was: should Ms. Ackley have directly warned the buyers about the hauntedness of the house beforehand instead of leaving it to chance whether or not they would discover this on their own.

This matter reached the New York Appellate Division of the Supreme Court on July 18, 1991. After all of the particulars had been presented before the justices - who were hearing this on appeal - the presiding judge, Justice Rubin, issued his statement, which follows word for word as it was announced.

BY JUSTICE RUBIN

The usual facts of the case, as disclosed by the record, clearly warrant a grant of equitable relief to the buyer who, as a resident of New York City, cannot be expected to have any familiarity with the folklore of the village of Nyack. Not being a "local" plaintiff could not readily learn that the home he had contracted to purchase is haunted. Whether the source of the spectral apparitions seen by the defendant seller are parapsychic or psychogenic, having reported their presence in both a national publication ("Reader's Digest") and the local press (in 1977 and 1982, respectively) defendant is stopped to deny their existence and, AS A MATTER OF LAW, THE HOUSE IS HAUNTED (authors highlights).

Those were the exact words of an appellate level judge on the New York Supreme Court: "As a matter of law, the house is haunted."

But Justice Rubin had more to say, as follows.

...in 1989, the house was included in a five-home walking tour of Nyack and described in a November 27th newspaper article as a "river front Victorian (with ghost)." ...a fair reading of the merger clause reveals that it expressly disclaims only representations made with respect to the physical conditions of the premises and merely makes general references concerning "any other matter or things affecting or relating to the aforesaid premises." As broad as this language may be, a reasonable interpretation is that its effect is limited to tangible or physical

accordance with her obligation under the provisions of the contract rider. In the case at bar, defendant seller deliberately fostered the belief that her home was possessed. Having undertaken to inform the public at large, to whom she has no legal relationship, about the supernatural occurrences on her property, she may be said to owe no less...to her contract vendee.

In other words: Ms. Ackley should have plainly and directly informed the Stambovsky's about the spirit that was terrorising her house. She'd told just about everyone else she met - why not them? Could it be that she was afraid that they might not want to buy a haunted house?

The major argument against this view is: shouldn't the Stambovsky's have found

out this information on their own? After all, the haunting of the house they were about to buy was well publisized in the "Reader's Digest" and had been prominently featured on a walking tour as a haunted house. The justices didn't view the matter this way. What follows is the written legal conclusion.

Haunting of home is not a condition which can and should be ascertained upon reasonable inspection of the premises by the purchaser.

Equity would permit purchaser to rescind contract for sale of home and recover his down payment upon discovery of the home's reputation as being haunted.

Judgement (sic), Supreme Court, New York

County (Edward H. Lehner, J.) entered April 9, 1990, modified on the law and the facts and in exercise of discretion and the first cause of action seeking recission of the contract reinstated, without costs.

- **OFFICIAL VERDICT:** *The house was declared legally haunted, the contract of the sale was voided, and the down payment was ordered returned to the purchasers.*

CLOSING STATEMENT

There is a very clear and a very distinct difference between the types of ghosts and other spirits which haunt houses as opposed to the types of ghosts or spirits which return to this plane to either exact justice for crimes having been committed against them or to assist those in need of help in dealing with confusing or lost wills or with other financial aid.

While all of these entities are ghosts, they represent decidedly different species of ghost. Ghosts who have returned to exact one form of justice or another are of a clearly consciously driven nature. They can be seen and very often also heard. And once their mission is completed, they depart and are never to be seen or heard from again.

Note the type of ghost who haunts houses or other locations of a physical nature. They throw things, cause noises and can be general nuisances or terrifying spectres. These types of spirits are bound to a particular location.

Occasionally the species of ghost who haunts a location can also be of the type which has returned to exact justice. Perhaps their bodies had been secretly buried in the house. Perhaps they were the murderers and were bound to the location until they revealed their crime.

There are many varieties of ghost in existence. One thing they all have in common - their existence has been verified by the official proceedings of courts of law!

Treasure (sic)

VOLUME III – SPIRIT WILLS, TREAUSRE AND PHOTOGRAPHS

The format will be the same as in the previous two volumes.

DOCKET # C1 (1774) THE WILL OF MAJOR BLOMBERG
Wills and Ghosts, 465

Two British officers who were stationed in the American colonies were visited by the ghost of a fellow officer one evening while they sat together in their tent. The ghost did not enter the tent but spoke to them from the outside, giving the men directions where to locate a will that he had hidden in his home in England just before leaving for the colonies. The ghost requested that they see to it that the will was properly executed upon their return to England.

- **POINT OF SIGNIFICANCE:** *The two officers were visited by Major Blomberg AFTER he had died. They weren't aware that they were speaking to a ghost. Neither of them had a personal interest in the will and - while it is possible that they could earlier have been told about it by the major - they could not have known about the officer's death BEFORE it occurred. Yet they did to speak to his ghost.*

- *Additionally, this is another of those very rare occasions were two people witness the same ghost at the same time.*

The two British officers were seated in their tent, waiting the arrival of Major Blomberg. The major had earlier gone on a foraging mission and his two compatriots were anxious for his return because they had made special dinner plans with him. It was with great relief that they heard the sound of the major's familiar footsteps. However, he did not enter the tent but remained outside and spoke to the two men from where he stayed, a voice that both clearly recognised.

The major implored the two men to attend to a very important item of business as soon as they returned to England. He directed them to go to a certain house in Westminster where they were to locate a specific box in which he had hidden some extremely important legal documents.

After giving the message, the major walked away; his familiar footsteps were as clearly recognised departing as they had been approaching. Why was he leaving! They had a special dinner planned that was to celebrate their return to England!

The two officers leapt to the exit of the tent and burst outside. There wasn't anyone there. Major Blomberg was nowhere to be seen.

The officers hurried to a nearby sentry who was on watch. They questioned him about the major. He told them that no one had been in the area and he certainly would have noticed an officer of the rank of Major Blomberg.

The two men returned to their tent, utterly bewildered. A short time later, their bewilderment changed to naked shock. A fellow officer entered the tent and gave them the horrible news of the death of Major Blomberg. He'd been killed while foraging with his men and his body had been returned to camp not more than ten minutes before.

The time frame placed the death of Major Blomberg as occurring at approximately the moment that he was conversing with the two officers in the tent.

Upon returning to England, among the first actions performed by the two officers was to seek out the house to which the major had directed them. They conducted a search of the room designated and found an old tin box in which lay hidden the title deed to valuable property in Yorkshire. No one else knew that the strongbox even existed.

There already had been major disputes raging among members of Major Blomberg's family as to the identity of the genuine heir to his estate. It was through the intercession of the major's ghost on that dark night in distant America that the matter was settled.

The major had named his only son the true heir. Not only was this specified in the legal papers in the concealed strongbox but also revealed was the existence of the property in Yorkshire of which no one had know.

DOCKET # C2 (1910) NURSE V. STATE 128 S.W. 906

59 TEX CRIM. 354

James Nurse entered into an agreement with Mr. Alexander calling for him to locate for him buried treasure in his yard for a small fee. Money was found by Mr. Nurse per the bargain, but he later stole the money and was taken to court by the aggrieved and charged with swindling. James Nurse was convicted on these charges but filed an appeal.

· **POINT OF SIGNIFICANCE:** *According to all accounts, Mr. Nurse was led to the site of the buried money by spirits and was successful finding "treasure" for Mr. Alexander on more than one occasion using ghostly guides.*

This is an extremely confusing and convoluted case. It begins when the Alexanders notice a group of round blue lights bobbing low over their front yard one dark night. This fact is little noted in the records and certainly is not given the importance it deserves.

In parapsychological terms, this type of observation has a specific meaning -

treasure is buried below the ground over which the lights are dancing.

The Alexanders most likely had an inkling of this. And it isn't stretching the bounds of credulity to think that James Nurse had also seen these lights and knew exactly what they meant. After all, the claimed to be a practicing spiritualist and as such would've understood this concept of buried treasure.

This also most likely is what led Mr. Nurse to approach the Alexanders with his proposition. He probably did not just randomly show up at their house with the offer to locate buried treasure for them and the Alexanders by the same logic were not shocked by what might otherwise have seemed an outrageous proposal.

The cleanest and clearest way to present this befuddling labyrinthine case is through testimony. What follows is a representation of the direct examination of Mr. Alexander - the aggrieved party. The testimony would have been from the original trial, at which Mr. Nurse sat accused of swindling the Alexanders.

BY THE PROSECUTION

Q. I'd like to ask you first, Mr. Alexander - are you a spiritualist.

A. No, I do not claim to be a spiritualist. But I am a student of folklore.

Q. I see. We'll take that up a little later. Now tell me, during the time in question, were having some type of work done on your home.

A. Yes, we were having the foundations shored up. We'd contracted Mr. Mabry to do the work.

Q. Was there something strange associated with this work.

A. Yes, at first my wife and I heard odd rappings coming from the front door threshold.

Q. Did you find the cause.

A. It wasn't from anything natural, if that's what you mean.

Q. Could you explain.

A. Well the noises were caused by the foundation settling, animals, the wind or running water.

Q. I see. Was there anything else strange that happened about this time.

A. Yes. That's when the ghost lights first appeared.

Q. What are ghost lights.

A. In this case they are roundish blue lights that hovered and bounced low to the ground.

Q. Where on your property were these lights.

A. Where the foundation had been dug up.

Q. Did the lights frighten you.

A. Just the opposite. Like I said, I'm a student of folklore and I know that lights like these usually dance over the spot where treasure is buried.

Q. Did you start digging for treasure then.

A. No. Didn't have to. It was just at this time that Mr. Nurse - the defendant - showed up and told me that he could contact the spirits and they would direct him right to where the treasure was buried.

Q. Would he do this free of charge.

A. No. There would be a fee.

Q. How much.

A. Twenty dollars. Half of it was to be paid when he started digging and the rest when he found whatever it was that was buried in the ground.

Q. Did you agree to this.

A. Sure. It seemed I had little to lose.

Q. What happened next.

A. Mister Nurse toured my property and stopped where my wife and I had seen the ghost lights. He said that this is where money was buried.

Q. Did he start digging.

A. Yes. Even Mr. Mabry the construction foreman stood and watched him. Actually, Mr. Mabry had already found a big cedar block deep in the ground and also suspected there was money down there somewhere.

Q. Did Mr. Nurse find any money.

A. Yes. He found $42.00 in gold coins in a small pit.

Q. Did he give you this money.

A. Not directly. He put the money into a tin can and gave the can to my wife.

Q. What did she do with it.

A. This is the strange part. He had my wife carry the can of coins to back yard where Mr. Nurse then re-buried it in front of the three of us.

Q. Why did he re-bury the coins.

A. Mister Nurse told me that if the money were physically handled in any other way than we had that the spirits would make it vanish and would not use this money to help us find more money.

Q. More money.

A. Yes, the plan was to find more money.

Q. I'm curious about something else - why did the defendant have *your wife* carry the money to the back yard. Why not you or Mr. Mabry.

A. Mister Nurse explained that. He said that having a female transport the money made the process more like the offering of a sacrifice to the spirits of the earth.

Q. Okay, let's recap a little here. This is a rather complicated procedure. The defendant found the $42.00, placed it in a tin can, had your wife carry it to the back yard, where he then buried this tin can in hopes that the spirits would then lead him to the location of even more money.

A. That is correct.

Q. Did you find more money.

A. Yes. That same evening.

Q. Tell us about it.

A. It was early evening and the defendant had come back to our house after having dinner and taking a rest. He led my wife and I to a spot near the front of our house that was not far from where were found the first pit of money.

Q. Did he dig there.

A. Yes. This time he found a whole bucketful of what appeared to be gold coins. My wife and I were pretty excited.

Q. Did you examine any of the coins.

A. Yes, Mr. Nurse handed my wife and I each a coin from the top of the pile.

Q. Did Mr. Nurse also insist on burying this find as well.

A. Yes, he did. It was hard to let him bury so much money, but we agreed.

Q. Where did he bury it.

A. Near the front stoop.

Q. Did he have your wife carry the bucket.

A. No, he didn't.

Q. Did you ask him why not.

A. No, it never occurred to me.

Q. Didn't it seem peculiar that in the first instance it was important for your wife to carry the money before reburial but not in the second instance.

A. Like I said - the question never occurred to me.

Q. What happened after the defendant buried the bucketful of coins.

A. He told us not to touch anything and that he would be back in the morning to locate even more money and this time we would keep it all.

Q. Is that what happened.

A. No. We never saw the defendant again until we had him arrested for swindling us.

Q. Why do you believe he swindled you. Didn't he locate buried money as he promised.

A. He located it all right. But he also stole it.

Q. Why do you claim that.

A. Because when the defendant did not reappear the next morning my wife and I checked the back yard where the original find of money had been buried and it was gone. The same coins were later found in Mr. Nurse's possession.

Q. Despite all of what you have just told us, I understand that there is something mitigating that you would like to directly address to the court.

A. Yes.

Q. Proceed.

At this point, Mr. Alexander spoke directly to the judge, putting forth an offer. What follows are his EXACT words.

with iron washers as those common in railroad yards of the day.

In the original case James Nurse was convicted of swindling Mr. Alexander. However, the case was appealed and overturned. The defenndant would've been found guilty of theft, but he wasn't charged with theft. And he couldn't be convicted of swindling because he DID fill his part of the bargain with Mr. Alexander which was to locate buried treasure for him.

· **OFFICIAL APPELLATE COURT VERDICT:** *We are of the opinion that the evidence does not support the conviction. If appellant (Nurse) made the representations that he was a Spiritualist and could talk with spirits, this matter raised the question about which this court does not feel to be called upon or decide. There is no evidence in regard to the matter, one way or the other, that is, as to whether or not the appellant conversed with spirits, or called them up and tested their veracity, but the fact is uncontroversial, whether he talked with spirits or not, that he found the money as he promised.*

But HOW did he find the money. Somehow he knew where to look, and the money was there where he dug. And the second digging raised only a bucketful of railroad washers.

It seemed a clear case of deception. But, then again, not so clear.

If the original find was money Mr. Nurse had "planted" it had to have been his own money - $42.00 worth. His charge for

)))

digging up the $42.00 was twenty dollars. If the buried money was his own it would seem the scheme would have COST him $22.00!

Unless Mr. Nurse were insane it didn't seem likely that the $42.00 he found was really his own. Which leaves the prospect that he was actually led to this money by spirits and that the discovery of it was truly by supernatural methods.

But if this were the case - where did the bucketful of railroad washers come from? This was dug up by Mr. Nurse, too.

Had it been mischievous elves that led Mr. Nurse to the bucketful of washers? If so, why did Mr. Nurse trick the Alexander's with the two gold coins from the top of the heap of washers?

All of this just so that he could come back in the night and reclaim the $42.00 he'd left buried in the back yard! It is true, however, that Mr, Nurse would have come away with a profit of $20.00 upon collecting his finders fee.

This seems an awfully difficult way to make $20.00, probably all of which would've been taken up by lawyer's fees.

CONCLUSION:?

DOCKET # C3 (1910) CRAVEN V CRAVEN 103 N.E. 333

Appealed Indiana Supreme Court

The ghost of Jasper Barker appeared to his nephew and revealed the existence of a long lost will that would have been of great benefit to the nephew, Jasper Craven. The court ruled that the statute of limitations had expired on probating the will. Jasper Craven argued that the statute of limitations should only have gone into affect upon discovery of the will and he appealed the ruling.

· **POINT OF SIGNIFICANCE:** *Jasper Craven could not have known of the existence of the will without supernatural intervention. The only other living person who knew of the will's existence had long forgotten it and was unknown to Jasper Craven. Jasper could not seek out the whereabouts of a will from a person he could not have known existed except through information supplied by the ghost of his uncle.*

When Jasper Barker died at his home on December 13, 1864 from wounds inflicted during the War Between the States no one in this family knew that he had drawn up a will. His kinfolk simply remained on the land - his land - where they had lived and divided ownership of it according to their order of relationship to the deceased.

The official courtroom records tell the story of Jasper Barker's demise and Jasper Craven's legal suit best, therefore this is what will be presented next exactly as it appears.

The appellee (Jasper Craven) is the oldest son of
Adeline Barker Craven and W. M. craven and was
born on this land November 1863, and was named for
his Uncle Jasper.

Jasper barker enlisted in the army with others
of the neighbourhood, among which were Enoch Scotten
And F.M. York, both of whom lived near the Barkers.
Jasper Barker was wounded in battle and in September
1864, was in a hospital in Marietta, Ga.. From
there he was sent home on furlough. He died at
his home on the land in controversy December 13, 1864.
Enoch Scotten was also home on furlough when Jasper
died and had visited him two or three times during
his last illness. After the war, Scotten and York

returned to that vicinity and lived there until 1879
when York removed to Kansas, where he died some years
ago, Scotten continued to live in the neighbourhood
until 1909.

The appellee lived with his mother, the appellant,
until he was 24 years old or until 1887. Neither
he nor Jane barker nor appellant had any knowledge
of the existence of any will made by Jasper Barker
until in the spring of 1909, when as appellee claims,
his uncle Jasper Barker, although having been dead

for more than 44 years appeared to him in a vision,

or dream, and told him of the existence of a will

and that it was in the possession of Enoch Scotten,

who still lived in the neighbourhood, and who upon

the request of the appellee produced and gave him

the will.

These are the official court records. When Jasper Craven was called to testify he had a very interesting story to tell and what follows is substantially what he said.

BY THE DEFENCE ATTORNEY

Q. You claim to have been visited by your late uncle in a dream?

A. Well, it was more of a vision, I'd say. That's because I had it during the day. I wasn't really sleeping, but sort of dozing.

Q. Did your uncle speak to you.

A. Yes. He told me that he wanted me to have the land that was his. He seemed confused why I wasn't master of it.

Q. This may sound a strange question, but - did your uncle know that he had passed on.

A. Yes, he knew. But he only just knew.

Q. Can you explain that.

A. He said that it was like he'd just woke up from bed after a long sleep.

Q. He didn't know that almost 45 years had passed.

A. No. He knew he had died, but he thought it was just recent.

Q. Why was he sure now that he was dead.

A. He saw his old friend York. York is on the other side now and told Uncle Jasper what was happening.

Q. I see. So that's why it took your uncle so long to come back.

A. I reckon.

Q. Did he tell you why he didn't tell anyone about the will.

A. He did tell someone - York and Scotten.

Q. But why not anyone else.

A. Didn't trust anyone else. And I wasn't around yet to tell, or too young or something.

Q. So your uncle appeared to you in a vision. What did he actually say to you.

A. He told me that he'd writ up a will and in it he'd let me all his land. All of it.

Q. Where was the will.

A. Well, two people knew about it - York and Scotten - but it was Scotten who had the will now. He told me to go see him.

Q. Did you.

A. Soon as I could.

Q. Did he give you the will.

A. Sure did. Took his a little while to find it, but he was glad to give it to me.

Q. Why didn't he give it to you before - when your uncle died.

A That's a good question. I don't know. Probably because I was too young. Then he forgot about it, I reckon.

Q. Why didn't you go to him when your uncle died and ask him for it.

A. Because I ain't knew that the will was writ, remember. Couldn't ask for something if I didn't know about it. And remember - now that I figure things - I was just one year old when he died.

Q. I understand. I just wanted to make sure Judge Erwin knew this.

A. Right.

This essentially was what Jasper Craven had to say to the court on appeal. The case that ensued was between Jasper Craven and his mother Jane. Apparently they did not get along very well because they were now bitterly fighting over land on which they had been living together for many years.

Jasper's main argument was that since the will had not been found until recently the statute of limitations should not have begun until then. However, the statute of limitations began counting down in 1864, upon the death of Jasper Barker.

No one contested the validity of the will and the court even accepted the reality of the ghostly visitation by Jasper Craven's uncle. The ONLY question was when should the statute of limitations have begun running: in 1864 when Jasper Barker died or in 1909 when the will was revealed.

By the body of law that was used as precedent, the court of appeals decided that the statute of limitations began on the date of the testator's death which was December 13, 1864.

Judge Erwin took care to make a special note of the procrastination of the ghost of Jasper Barker in this affair.

While it may have been the intention of

the uncle to bestow upon the appellee the real

estate of which he died possessed, yet if he

had the power to appear to the nephew and

disclose the existence of the will in 1909, he is the only one who can be said to blame,

and his failure to make the facts known for

45 years had effectually barred the nephew's

right to recover.

That's right: it was the ghost's fault! Officially and under the law.

· **ADDITIONAL POINT OF SIGNIFICANCE:** *Two things must be remembered as factual evidence: 1)the nephew DID RECEIVE some form of*

——

paranormal message which told him of the existence of the will and, 2)the nephew also suddenly knew who had possession of the will. How did these things occur if not without supernatural intervention?

DOCKET # C4 (1901) DEAN V ROSS

178 Mass. 397, 60 N.E. 119

The plaintiff Ms. Dean sued the defendant Ms. Ross for the return of fifteen bonds which Ms. Dean claimed had been obtained by fraud. Acting a medium, Ms. Ross told Ms. Dean that Ms. Dean's

%%

departed husband wanted her to convey the fifteen bonds in question to Ms. Ross. Thinking that this was according to the desires of her late husband, Ms. Dean duly transferred possession of the bonds to Ms. Ross but later had misgivings.

- **POINT OF SIGNIFICANCE:** *the presiding judge in the matter - Judge Bond - instructed the jury to decide the matter of fraud based on whether or not they believed that the message had truly come from the deceased Mr. Dean and that it was honestly being forward as a genuine communication by the medium.*

The particulars are as they are and have just been stated. No one denies them. The defendant, Ms. Ross claimed that she was instructed by the spirit of the late Mr. Dean to tell his former wife that he wanted her to give the fifteen bonds to Ms. Ross. She said that this is what she honestly believed.

But what did the jury believe? Cases of fraud are always a difficult matter, especially when dealing with the supernatural. In this instance, however, the jurors felt that the defendant, Ms. Ross, was engaged in fraudulent behaviour rather than spiritualistic behaviour.

OFFICIAL VERDICT: *The defendant was ordered to return the fifteen bonds to the plaintiff, Ms. Dean.*

This seemingly innocent case is an important one. Important in that the judge recognised the potential of genuine communication with spirits of the deceased. It was right there in his instructions to the jury.

The judge did not discount such communication as delusional or in some way beyond reasonable possibility. In other words, the law conceded the point that communication with the dead is possible.

DOCKET # C5 (1895) MCCLARY V. STULL
44. Neb. 175., 62 N.W. 501

The plaintiff McClary sought to have the will of the defendant Stull deemed incompetent on the grounds that Ms. Stull prepared the document under the influence of her deceased husband's spirit. The Court disagreed and allowed

---

the will to stand. The verdict was appealed.

· **POINT OF SIGNIFICANCE:** *Once again this is a matter where the Court stated its position in favour of the possibility of communication with spirits of the deceased.*

The observations of the Court in general follow this viewpoint: there is nothing improper with a person putting faith in communication with spirits of departed loved ones, however, the situation becomes more troublesome when a third party such as a medium becomes part of the equation.

What follows are the remarks made by three different judges concerning three

****
****

different cases all of which involved the competency of a will that was prepared under the auspices of a former loved one's spirit.

FIRST OPINION

It is entirely legitimate and proper for the wife to seek the advice of her living husband, and after death to pay some regard to his known wishes in the preparation of her will; but when such pretended counsel comes through the dubious channel of a 'medium,' as an oracle from one possessing knowledge of the great hereafter, under the solemn surroundings of the séance, its influence upon a credulous mind can hardly be measured. *Steinkuehler v. Wempner, 81 N.E. 482 (1907)*.

SECOND OPINION

Law, it is said, is 'of the earth, earthy,' and spirit-wills are too celestial for cognisance by earthly tribunals, - a proposition readily conceded; and yet the courts have not assumed to deny the spirits of the departed the privilege of holding communion with those of their friends who are still in the flesh so long as they do not interfere with vested rights or by the means of undue influence seek to prejudice the interests of persons still within our jurisdiction. *McClary v. Stull, 44 Neb. 175, (1895)*.

THIRD OPINION

^^^
^^^^^^^^^^^^^^^

If there was a message received from the husband, and the defendant simply delivered the message, believing it to be true, to this plaintiff, why then that would not be any false statement with reference to the transaction; that would be a true statement, and I meant you to understand that then the plaintiff could not recover, if that was a fact and that was a real communication. *Dean v. Ross, 178 Mass. 397 (1901).*

All of which leads back to the case at hand, the competency of the Stull will. Even though it was known that Ms. Stull consulted her deceased husband's spirit through use of planchette and was a practicing spiritualist, the jury found her to be competent and qualified to execute her own will and allowed it to stand.

OFFICIAL VERDICT: *Mrs. Stull was competent when she devised her will under the auspices of the spirit of her deceased husband.*

Early American Spiritualism pp 304-305.

DOCKET # C6 (ca 1899) IRA B. EDDY SPRITUALIST BANK

Ira B. Eddy was a wealthy man who lived in Chicago, Illinois during the later portion of the 19th century and the early part of the 20th century. He was a devoted Spiritualist and through the

---

inspiration of spirits founded a bank in Chicago along with several other like-minded men of wealth. His brother - D.C. Eddy - feared that Ira was going to dissipate the family fortune and had him declared incompetent by a local tribunal.

POINT OF SIGNIFICANCE: *The belief in Spiritualism was considered by many people during this age to be a sign of delusional thinking and clinical insanity. Importantly, Ira B. Eddy had both the monetary and psychological support of many other prominent Chicagoans to aid in the fight against such prejudicial judgments.*

The banking institution that Ira Eddy founded was not a simple fly-by-night operation. It was a genuine

)))

)))))))))))))))))))))))

institution which adhered to all of the applicable banking laws and possessed a considerable portfolio of negotiable assets.

The officers who ran this program along with Mr. Eddy were all successful businessmen and professional people, including the postmaster for the Chicago region. And they were all Spiritualists. They believed in communication with the spirits of the departed and sought their advice in investment opportunities. This was a fact which anyone who did business with this bank was aware of. No one was coerced to participate in this particular system of banking which was completely legal, and , in fact, successful. Ira's bother D.C. was also a powerful personage, however. He used his considerable influence to have his brother face a sanity hearing, during which D.C. claimed that Ira was not capable of handling his affairs and that control of his assets should be turned over to him. The members who sat on the board agreed and found Ira Eddy incompetent. Not surprisingly, D.C. Eddy was made conservator of the Eddy estates.

Afterward, D.C. took the initiative and has his brother forcibly removed to an asylum for the insane in another state.

Ira's partners in his banking firm were alarmed at these developments and appealed the matter before a state court. It was a regular court that heard the matter on this occasion and ruled in favour of Ira Eddy.

---

of his property or one quarter of the proceeds of the sale of his property upon his death. James Harris, brother of Thomas, was named executor of the will and as such was to carry out Thomas's wishes. James failed to do so. Instead, he sold his brother's property and kept the money himself.

· **POINT OF SIGNIFICANCE:** *The ghost of Thomas Harris appeared on several occasions in order to have the wishes of his will carried out. The ghost's statements to his friend William Briggs were repeated in open court by Mr. Briggs and are an official part of the court documents.*

The following action took place in Queen Ann's County in Maryland in the year 1798. The United States had just passed its 20th birthday , John Adams was president, and the courts were still relying heavily on English case law for precedents. In fact, the decision in the case involving Major Blomberg's will was used as one of the precedents for deciding this cause of action.

This trial is of particular importance because much of the evidence is taken from a witness's conversations with a ghost. An invaluable first-hand account of the proceedings was supplied by the detailed notes made by one of the counsels trying this affair, Joseph H. Nicholson, esquire.

It is also of particular interest that the other counsellor was a former governor of Maryland, Robert Wright.

Although the notes of the proceedings are detailed they do not make any attempt at explanation or interpretation. For example, what follows is a an abstract of the dynamics of the case:

It appears that Thomas Harris made some alteration
in the disposal of his property immediately previous
to his death; and that the family disputed the will
and raised up difficulties likely to be injurious
to his children.

Note the lack of mention of the ghost which played so prominent a part of the trial that ensued.

The ghost of Thomas Harris appeared almost exclusively to his friend, William Briggs. Harris and Briggs served together in the American War for Independence

++
++++++++++++++

and had been very close. It isn't any wonder that Harris chose him to whom to appear when he sought to have the wishes of his will made known and put into force.

The most telling aspect of the trial was the testimony of the primary witness, William Briggs, which here follows substantially as it would have appeared. None of the circumstances or facts have been altered.

BY THE DEFENCE ATTORNEY

Q. Your name is William Briggs.

A. Yes.

Q. Did you serve with the deceased, Thomas Harris, during the Revolutionary War.

A. Yes, I did.

Q. Would you consider yourselves close.

===
===============

A. As close as brithers(sic).

Q. The ghost of Thomas Harris has appeared to you.

A. Many times.

Q. Do you remember the first time he appeared to you.

A. Not rightly so because the first times I wasn't sure what it was.

Q. Can you explain that.

A. Well I one time heard a groaning coming from nowhere. And another time I was given this clout on the nose by a hand that wasn't there.

Q. And you assumed that these were signs from the ghost of Thomas Harris.

A. Well, later I did, after I started seeing the true ghost.

Q. Was James Harris - Thomas's brother - still alive at this time.

A. Yes, when I first started seeing the ghost he was. One of the things the ghost wanted me to do was to tell his brother to remember what his will said - that his kids were to share his property.

Q. Tell us about this meeting with the ghost.

A. Well, it was more like three different meetings. I first saw the ghost in one of the fields that used to belong to him. But then he vanished. A little while later, he appeared again and this time came and leaned on the fence railing.

Q. Was there anyone else there at the time.

A. Yep, a boy who helps us out with the farm work - name's Bailey.

Q. Did he see the ghost.

A. No. As much as I tried to make him see it - he couldn't.

Q. All right - so you left off with the ghost of Thomas Harris leaning on the fence railing.

A I went toward him but he disappeared again.

Q. What happened next.

A. A little bit more time passed and then the ghost showed up again, this time out in the middle of the field.

Q. What did you do.

A. Bailey was still there and I tried to make him see the ghost again. But he couldn't. So I climbed over the fence railing and walked out to the ghost. This is when I got to talk to him and I told him that his will was still in dispute.

Q. I see. And did the ghost answer you.

A Yup, this is when he told me to remind his brother about the private talk they had by the wheat-stacks.

\#

Q. Did you tell this to James Harris.

A. Yes. The ghost told me that it was really important that I remind James about the conversation they'd had that day on the east side of the wheat-stacks. It was the same day that Jim came down with the sickness that kilt him.

Q. What did James Harris do when you told him about the message the ghost gave you.

A. Well at first he was pretty shocked. Nobody else knew about that conversation except him and his brother. He knew that the only way I could know about it is if I was telling the truth about the ghost. He knew it.

Q. Do you recall when was the next time that you actually saw the ghost of Thomas Harris.

===
============

A. Yes, it was sometime in March, 1791. It was about nine in the morning.

Q. Can you tell us about it.

A Sure. I was riding a horse that used to belong to Tom.

Q. Mister Harris.

A. Right. Tom Harris. It was his horse I was riding. And I was riding down the lane that was right by the field where Tom was buried.

Q. What happened.

A. The horse got all agitated. It shied and neighed and stood still there in the middle of the road.

Q. Do you know why.

A. Sure. It was Tom's ghost. He was wearing his usual blue jacket and came walking toward us right through the field. Then - as suddenly as he came -

----
----

he vanished. And the horse got back to normal again and we rode off.

It is important to note that animals, and particularly horses, are very susceptible to the paranormal. This would apply doubly so to this particular event since the ghost that was seen used to be the master of the horse in question.

Additionally, the location is of vital importance. The horse became agitated BEFORE the ghost became visible. After all, the burial plot of his former master was in the field nearby.

These matters bear noting because some people had claimed that William Briggs had been perpetrating a hoax. But the facts do not bear this out. The locations and times where he sees the ghost agree perfectly with what is known to occur during encounters with the supernatural; such as where, when and why the horse that had belonged to the deceased acted as it did.

Another fact that points away from the hoax theory is how desperately Mr. Briggs tried to get the young Mr. Bailey to see the same ghost that he was seeing that day in the field. This is the sign of man who is in earnest. If Briggs were simply a man making things up, he really wouldn't care if anyone else saw his "imagine" ghost or not. Bailey's upcoming testimony will make this clearer.

Resuming with the testimony of William Briggs by the defence attorney:

Q. When did you next see the ghost of Thomas Harris.

A. I saw him one last time, but I'm not exactly sure of the date on this.

Q. What happened on this occasion.

A. This I cannot reveal.

Q. I don't understand.

A. The matter that was discussed on this meeting between the ghost and me was of a highly personal nature which the ghost said I should tell no one.

Q. You are expected to tell the WHOLE truth in a court of law, Mr. Briggs. Not only the truth which is convenient to you.

A. That might be, but there are matters that should not be spoken of in public. Nothing short of life will make me tell what passed between the ghost and me that day.

JUDGE TO WITNESS

Q. As I understand it, Mr Briggs, you are claiming protection of the court.

A. Yes, your honour.

Q. Mr. Briggs, do you avow that you have told this court everything that you know relative to this case.

A. I do.

Q. Then the court grants its protection from further examination. You may stand down.

With that stormy conclusion, the testimony of William Briggs was completed.

The notes taken by Mr. Nicholoson of this episode are quite compelling and follow verbatim.

The counsel was extremely anxious to hear from

Mr. Briggs the whole of the conversation with the ghost, and on his cross-examination took every means, without effect, to obtain it. They represented to him, as a religious man, he was bound to disclose the whole truth. He appeared agitated when applied to, declaring nothing short of life should make him reveal the whole conversation, and, claiming the protection of the court, that he had declared all he knew relative to the case.

There was yet one more witness of note to be heard from, albeit very briefly: young Mr. Bailey. He was called to the stand and what follows is essentially what he told the court.

BY THE DEFENCE ATTORNEY
Q. You are the Bailey who Mr. Briggs spoke about as having accompanied him during a couple of his ghost sightings.
A. Yes, I am.
Q. Did the matter take place as Mr. Briggs described.
A. Yes. I was walking along with him alongside the field when Mr. Briggs suddenly became all agitated.
Q. Did he say why he was agitated.
A. Yes, he said that he saw the ghost of Tom Harris walking through the nearby field.

Q. Did you see the ghost.

A. No, I saw nothing.

Q. Did Mr. Briggs try to get you to see the ghost.

A. Yes. He kept pointing in that direction and turning me toward it to be able to see.

Q. Did you ever see anything there.

A. No. from what I could tell there was nothing to see.

Q. from what I understand, the ghost disappeared and then reappeared.

A. That's what Mr. Briggs claims.

Q. Did he try to help you see it the second time.

A. Yes. But I still couldn't see the ghost.

Q. Did Mr. Briggs then leave the road and go off into the field.

A. Yes, he climbed through - between the fence rails - and went off into the field.

Q. Was he alone.

A. That's hard to say.

Q. Why.

A. I didn't see anyone with him, but he was sure acting like there was someone there with him.

Q. Acting. How.

A. He was walking on and on and as he walked he seemed to be talking to someone. And he was gesturing a lot. I swear it looked like he was talking to someone. But I couldn't see who.

The testimony of Mr. Bailey is quite telling. Taking into account Mr. Briggs' actions, he gave every appearance of speaking to someone as he walked through the field. This is important because it shows intent. A person engaged in a hoax ordinarily would not have been as convincing as was Mr. Briggs. Just because Bailey could not see who Briggs was talking to does not necessarily mean that there wasn't anyone there. Some people can't see ghosts.

The basic facts of the case have been presented. The court did not accept the argument that Mr. Briggs had been engaged in a hoax. Further, the court accepted his testimony and gave the weight of admissible evidence to the words of the ghost which were relayed by Mr. Briggs.

- **OFFICIAL VERDICT:** *The wishes of Thomas Briggs were to be upheld and his four children were to each receive one quarter of the value of his property.*

DOCKET # C8 (1869) CITY OF NEW YORK V. MUMLER

In 1869 the City of New York charged a photographer named Mumler with fraud for claiming to be able to produce photographs which contained images of spirits of the deceased. He would be the first of many to be tried on this type of offence.

- **POINT OF SIGNIFICANCE:** *While taking a photograph of a patron in October 1862 Mumler discovered another figure on the photographic plate. The other face belonged to a cousin of the patron, the cousin having died twelve years before.*

This was the innocent birth of spirit photography.

· At the time. Mumler was a beginning photographer in Boston. Massachusetts. Photography was in its earliest stage of development, having only recently been legitimatised as a science.

News of the spirit photograph that appeared on the same photograph as that of Mumler's patron Dr. Gardner spread rapidly throughout the spiritualist world. Patrons hoping to see photographs of their deceased friends and loved ones deluged Mumler's studio.

There was soon, trouble. In February of 1863, Mumler's original patron - Dr. Gardner - noticed that in at least two of the so-called spirit photographs living people had sat in for the supposed ghosts.

Oddly, this did not put an end to Mumler's business. Doctor Gardner and many of the other believers chose to accept a little fraud as long as some of the photographs were genuine.

It is important to note that the production process of most of the photographs was closely supervised by other experts in photography.

Mumler eventually left Boston and started a studio in New York City. He resumed the business of spirit photography. However, various officials who worked for the city of New York were suspicious of him and brought charges of fraud against him within weeks of the opening of his studio. This was in 1869.

A trial was held, but the prosecution was not allowed to present evidence of fraud which was available from Mumler's days in Boston. Additionally, the defence called many satisfied witnesses to testify in Mumler's behalf.

Several photographers were also questioned by the defence as expert witnesses for Mumler's cause and all of them stated that they could not discover the slightest hint of trickery in his process.

There wasn't any substantial evidence produced by the prosecution against Mr. Mumler. Apparently someone in the New York district attorney's office had been threatened by the spiritualistic aspects of Mumler's photography and decided to wage a personal vendetta against him.

- **OFFICIAL VERDICT:** *All charges against Mr. Mumler were dismissed due to lack of evidence.*

Mumler was free to resume his business of providing photographs of spirits. But one has to wonder how free of harassment he was from the overly eager city officials.

Proces des Spirites, by M. Leymarie

In June of 1875 the Government of France arrested and put on trial for fraud the Parisian photographer Buguet. He was charged with falsifying spirit photographs.

DOCKET # C9 (1875) FRANCE V. BUGUET

===
============

POINT OF SIGNIFICANCE: *Although Buguet had a very strong defence, including numerous witnesses and a lengthy series of photographic plates whose validity was not disputed, he chose to plead guilty. His willingness to confess so fully and without reservation is one of the enduring mysteries of this trial.*

The trial of Buguet was a great affair not only in Paris but throughout the world. Spiritualists were drawn to this courtroom from all over the globe. So too was a large contingent of the more traditional clergy who sought to safeguard their beliefs.

During this era, traditional religion was greatly threatened by Spiritualism and actively tried to eradicate this threat. Buguet was one of their biggest targets.

It has been suggested that much of the incriminating evidence against Buguet had been planted or manufactured by the clergy. It has also been suggested that Buguet's confession was coerced and that he was responding to threats made against him by the Church. In any event, there isn't any direct evidence in support of these accusations.

A very long line of witnesses marched to the stand in support of Buguet. Many of them were famous people. One of the most important was an expert in photography named W. H. Harrison.

Harrison had examined Buguet's photographic process for the Court and was called upon as an expert witness to give his evaluation. What follows is a representation of his testimony.

BY THE DEFENCE ATTORNEY

Q. You are W. H. Harrison.

A. I am.

Q. What is your profession.

A. I am a photographer.

Q. Do you produce spirit photographs.

A. No, that is not my expertise.

Q. As I understand it, you have been called upon by this court to examine the defendant's photographic techniques and to act as a person with expert knowledge in these matters.

A. That is correct.

Q. While observing Buguet in his preparation of the photographic plates through the various stages did you at any time witness any suspicious behaviour.

A. No. I did not find any indication whatsoever of fraud or trickery.

Q. Would you classify the so-called spirit photographs he has taken as genuine.

A. Yes, I would.

Q. Do any of these photographs stand out in your mind so that you can give a description of what method you used to determine their authenticity.

A. Yes. The photos of Allan Kardec come to mind. When Mr. Kardec's widow was sitting for her portrait the exact likeness of Mr. Kardec appeared with hers on the plate.

Q. Would his widow agree with your finding - that it was Mr. Kardec's likeness.

A. Certainly. She was the one who verified it for me.

Q. I noted that earlier you spoke about the photos of Mr, Kardec in the plural. Was there more than one likeness of his that appeared among the plates you studied.

A. Yes. His likeness also appeared when the sitter was Anna Blackwell.

Q. Why do you suspect he appeared with her as well as with his widow.

A. Miss Blackwell was one of Mr. Kardec's most loyal disciples, a strong proponent of Spiritism.

Q. Now this is very important - was the likness of Kardec that appeared on the plate with his widow the same likeness that appeared with Miss Blackwell. What I mean - as if it was an exact copy.

A. No. It was a likeness of Mr. Kardec but in a different pose and with different lighting and background.

Q. Miss Blackwell sat for other photographs did she not.

A. Yes. The likeness of Judge Edmonds - a very prominent Spiritualist in America - appeared on the plate.

Q. Did Stainton Moses take part in any of these photographic experiments.

A. Yes, one of the most startling. Mister Moses is one of the recognised leaders of the Spiritualist movement and he was eager to participate.

Q. What was his contribution.

A. He telepathically transmitted an image of himself to one of Buguet's sensitised photographic plates while remaining in his led in London in a deep trance.

Q. All the way from London to Paris.

A. Yes.

Q. What were the results.

A. A perfect likeness was captured.

Q. Did Mr. Moses play any other part in the ongoing investigation.

A. Yes, he examined about 120 of the photographs in question and found that there were at least forty recognisable portraits on them.

Q. And these are portraits of ordinary people.

A. Yes, portraits of ordinary people who were recognised by friends and relatives.

These forty portraitures were highly significant. While it would not have been exceptionally difficult to fraudulently reproduce the features of well known personages, it would have been exceedingly more difficult to reproduce the features of friends or relatives of average people who would randomly come to the studio for a sitting.

Yet that is what Buguet did time after time after time. And witness after witness appeared on the witness stand to testify to this fact.

What follows is a verbatim portion of courtroom testimony highlighting the judge questioning both a witness and Buguet.

WITNESS: The portrait of my wife, which I had specially asked for, is so like her that when I showed it to one of my relatives he exclaimed, 'It's my cousin.'

THE COURT: Was that chance, Buguet?

BUGUET: Yes, pure chance. I had no photograph of Mme. Dessenon.

WITNESS: My childen, like myself, thought the likeness perfect. When I showed them the picture, they cried, 'It's mamma.' A very fortunate chance! I am convinced it is my wife.

At this point the judge motions to several items that had been brought into court as physical exhibits. He addresses the witness.

THE COURT: You see this doll and all the rest of the things?

WITNESS: There is nothing there in the least like the photograph which I obtained.

THE COURT: You may stand down.

What did Buguet have to say when he was called to the stand? Nothing but self-incrimination. Following is a representation of his testimony.

BY THE PROSECUTING ATTORNEY

Q. You deny that any of the photographs are real.

A. They were all created by use of double exposure.

Q. Did you have help perpetrating this fraudulent scheme.

A. At first I used three or four assistants. I had them dress up in various types of clothing and had them play the ghosts in the photographs.

Q. Did this method of trickery change later.

A. Yes, I became more popular than I had expected and was afraid that people would begin recognising the models who I had sitting in as ghosts. That's when I constructed featureless dolls to take their places. I found out what the clients expected to see and fashioned the dolls to look like what they expected.

Q. But there are a great many people as you've heard who deny the possibility that your photographs are fakes.

A. They are wrong.

Q. All of them.

A. Don't you think I should know better. After all, I made the pretend photographs.

It was impossible to wage a defence for a person so willing to fully confess to his own guilt. In fact, if the judge had been so inclined, he still could have found Buguet innocent, claiming that the defendant's own words of confession were incompetent. The judge chose not to do so.

Buguet even pointed out to the court a specific instance in which the fake photograph he had created was the same one used for three different clients. One client claimed that the portrait was of her mother, another client recognised it as her sister, and the third patron was certain that the face was that of a close friend.

However, maybe even that was a lie. Maybe Buguet made up that instance of the one feature standing in for three different people. But why?

According to Stainton Moses, the judge was biased and Buguet had either been terrorised or bribed by a Jesuit conspiracy to denounce his abilities as a medium and confess to his guilt.

The only person who could know the answer for certain is Buguet. And it appears that the only way to arrive at the truth is to convene a séance and put the question directly to the mysterious photographer.

OFFICIAL VERDICT: *Buguet was found guilty of perpetrating a fraud and was* *sentenced to one year in prison and fined 500 francs.*

DOCKET # C10 (1687) BOOTY V BARNABY
COURT OF THE KING'S BENCH

While attending a social function, the widow of Mr. Booty overheard Mr. Barnaby casually note that he and some friends actually saw 'Old Booty' run into the flames of hell. Widow Booty sued Barnaby for libel.

· **POINT OF SIGNIFICANCE:** *This is one of the most astonishing stories of the supernatural which has appeared before an open court of law. A large group of people literally saw a man being chased by demons into hell and kept logs about the observation.*

The legal proceedings can be found in the court of the King's Bench equity proceedings for 1687-88 and was also documented in a book titled, "Voyages up the Mediterranean," ii, 355 written by General Cockburn.

The date of the supernatural observation was Friday, May 15, 1687. Captains Barnaby, Bristow and Brown were hunting rabbits on the island of Stromboli. It was around four o'clock in the afternoon and all of the hunters and the beaters were gathered together near day's end.

All of a sudden they were disturbed by shouting and other noise. Everyone looked toward that direction and saw three men running toward them, but veering on a line toward where flames from a volcano were spouting out of the ground.

One man in particular was dressed in gray and black and was familiar to several in the hunting party. This man was leading the other two in the mad dash toward the flames.

"The foremost is Old Booty," observed Barnaby, "my next door neighbour."

And with that, the three figures disappeared into the volcanic flames.

Barnaby quizzed the two other ship's captains who were with him as to whether or not they had witnessed the same thing. They had. Barnaby insisted that they note this in their official ship logs, as would he. The other captains complied.

Then several months later came the night of the infamous dinner party. It was on October 6, 1687 at Gravesend and Barnaby, Bristol and Brown were there with their wives. The widow of Mr. Booty was on hand as well.

During the course of conversation, Mrs. Barnaby sadly remarked to her husband, "My dear, old Booty is dead."

The captain replied, "We all saw him run into hell."

Widow Booty was standing close enough to hear this remark and as a result sued Barnaby for libel, requesting damages in the amount of 1000 pounds.

The hearing was held. No one argued that Barnaby had not said what he said at the dinner party, how they had all seen Old Booty run into hell.

The only defence to libel is truth. If it could be proved that what Captain Barnaby had said was true, then he would be exonerated. How to prove that you'd seen your next door neighbour dash headlong into hell with two other souls?

The official ship's logs that had been kept at the time of occurrence were produced as evidence - all three logs. They all bore the same basic entry: *Friday, May 15, 1687, about four p.m. in the afternoon - Entire hunting party while on Stromboli witnessed a man known as Old Booty charge across the plain in the company of two other men and disappear into flames that were leaping up out of the ground.*

The year was 1687. This was well before the age of instant communication. The hunting party was far from the British Isles and no one on Stromboli could possibly have known of the death of Old Booty. They couldn't have learned of it for weeks. They were at sea.

Yet, the entries that were made in the logs were within minutes of the actual time of Booty's death. How else could they have possibly known of his death if they had not truly seen his apparition on that day as is described in the ship's logs?

There's more. The defence produced the clothing that Booty was wearing at the time of his death. It was singed! Singed as if by the fires of hell.

As unlikely as the defence of truth would apply in this case of libel, it was the best defence.

· **OFFICIAL VERDICT:** *Captain Barnaby was declared innocent of the charge of libel.*

THE END

www.ingramcontent.com/pod-product-compliance
Lightning Source LLC
Chambersburg PA
CBHW080051280326
41934CB00014B/3286

* 9 7 8 0 9 3 0 4 7 2 7 5 7 *